Communicating in Style

Yateendra Joshi

teri The Energy and Resources Institute

© The Energy and Resources Institute 2003

ISBN 81 7993 016 5

TERI	**Tel.** 2468 2100 or 2468 2111
Darbari Seth Block	**E-mail** outreach@teri.res.in
Habitat Place	**Fax** 2468 2144 or 2468 2145
Lodhi Road	**Web** www.teriin.org
New Delhi – 110 003	India +91 • Delhi (0) 11

Printed at Pauls Press, New Delhi

Contents

Foreword

Preface

Chapter 1 **Style for effective communication** 1
user-friendly, efficient, and distinct

2 **Heads, you win; text, I lose** 15
signposting documents with headings

3 **Make a list** 33
formatting and punctuating items in a series

4 **Alphabet soup** 47
abbreviations, acronyms, contractions, symbols

5 **How long is a piece of string?** 63
notation for units of measurement

6 **Setting the table** 75
presenting information in rows and columns

7 **Figures of speech** 103
charts, diagrams, maps, photographs

8 **Who said that?** 125
citing and formatting sources of information

9 **Remote control** 153
effective letters, faxes, and e-mails

10 **Stand and deliver** 165
making effective presentations

11 **Research on display** 179
designing effective posters

12 **Publish or perish** 187
submitting manuscripts to journals

13 **What's the point?** 205
Punctuation for clearer writing

Annexe A Specimen reference formats 215
B Authority for spellings 219
C Observing, choosing, and using fonts 225
D Postal and e-mail addresses and telephone numbers 231

Index 243

Foreword

by R K Pachauri, Director-General, T E R I

The production of this style guide would be a source of great satisfaction for those who are either involved themselves in producing technical literature or responsible for activities in organizations engaged in such work. I am aware of a major consulting organization that has been able to create an enviable record of success in dealing with the chief executives of major organizations around the world largely on the basis of a unique and appealing style of reports published by them. The multi-client reports that this organization produces are given much greater attention at the editing stage than perhaps even at the stage of collection of information, its organization and analysis, and on producing the contents of the basic subject matter itself. The last stages of finishing the product are the responsibility of the seniormost professionals in the organization. I mention this example only to highlight the fact that even with the richest content on the most esoteric subjects, the value of the final product can be diminished or enhanced substantially by the style of the publication. It is for this reason that a style guide is extremely important for enabling scientific writers in particular to come out with products that are not only scientifically valuable and rich in content, but attractive, interesting, and pleasing in all respects to the discriminating reader.

It is especially pertinent that my colleague Yateendra Joshi has worked on this particular product, because he not only brings to bear on this work knowledge, experience, and talent in designing published products, but a passion that provides a unique personality and utility to this guide. The pages that follow are not only full of insights and the distillation of his rich experience drawn from a wide range of publications, but also easy to read and remarkably simple to follow. Hence the message contained in this guide can be assimilated without any hardship or discomfort. For this and various other qualities, I think this style guide will make a valuable contribution in assisting the authors writing on a variety of subjects.

Preface

This book might as well have been titled 'Where there is no copy editor' – after David Werner's eminently successful book *Where There Is No Doctor* – because it is written mainly for those who must revise and polish their work on their own. Last year saw the publication of the 623-page *Oxford Guide to Style* and last month, the 984-page 15th edition of the *Chicago Manual of Style*. However, those tomes of distilled wisdom are for professional copy editors: if you are a researcher, an academic, a journalist, or a manager – long on technical expertise but short on time – you will find style manuals daunting and tedious. Yet, you may want to give your message that well-groomed look— *Communicating in Style* shows you how you can do that yourself.

The Energy and Resources Institute, the publisher of this volume, is an unusual research institute in many ways, one of them being that its researchers may choose to have their writing copy-edited by professionals. This book is a compilation of what those editors have learnt over the years from editing project reports, research papers, newsletters, presentations, manuals, posters, web pages: a variety of formats matched only by the variety of contents, which ranged from air pollution in rural kitchens to global climate change, from bacteria to forests, from policy-making to practical instruction in propagating plants.

The Director-General of TERI, R K Pachauri, suggested that I compile a style guide for in-house use. Accordingly, a draft version was prepared and circulated among TERI researchers and the staff of its information services, doctoral students at the TERI School of Advanced Studies, and many others outside TERI. That draft has now metamorphosed into this handbook, and I am grateful to all those who have had a hand in shaping it.

James Hartley, Chuck Hollingworth, Derek Land, Lynn P Nygaard, Elizabeth Orna, and Sue Walker read an early draft and offered comments or suggested improvements. Hal Cain, Carol Miller, and Elizabeth Wager did the same for several chapters. Conrad Taylor also commented on the design. Members of the Internet discussion groups devoted to copy-editing, typography, and information design patiently and promptly answered many queries.

At TERI, Vikram Dayal spoke for the prospective users of the book and helped in shaping it to serve their needs. P K Jayanthan, Nandini Kumar, Shehnaz Ahmed, and Amalesh Chakraborty diligently pored over successive versions of the text as Anshu Eashwar made the pages and T Radhakrishnan refined the typesetting and design. R K Joshi took all the pictures and offered helpful advice on the design of the left-hand pages. Supratim Chatterjee and Baldev Chand were instrumental in keeping me up to date with the latest books and periodicals. K P Eashwar's belief in the worth of the book despite its slow progress and Sangeeta Gupta's implicit faith in my judgement – on issues related to style – sustained me during this long journey—and the kind words of encouragement from John le Carré, M S Swaminathan, and Jean Hollis Weber made it worthwhile.

The shortcomings of the book are all of my own making, however: I apologize for them in advance and request the readers to point them out to me.

Chapter 1 at a glance

Why you should use this handbook
What is style and why it matters
Sources of advice and information
Developing a distinctive style
The essentials of style
- Keep in mind what the readers would find helpful instead of doing what is easiest for you
- Use abbreviations sparingly
- Choose larger fonts
- Prefer small letters to capital letters; use capitals only when you must
- Follow the *New Oxford Dictionary of English* in matters of spelling

References

1 ▶ Style for effective communication
user-friendly, efficient, and distinct

Now that you have managed to put your message down on paper, or saved it to a file in the computer, you have already accomplished the toughest part of any technical communication. This is true whether you are writing a letter, a report, an article for a magazine, or a research paper for a journal. All that remains is to dress the message up for the occasion so that its readers see it in the best possible light. It is when you begin to go over your draft carefully that you notice tiny (and at times not so tiny) flaws: the same word spelt with a hyphen in one place and without it elsewhere (by-product and byproduct); dates and time given in different formats (11 Sept. 2001 in one place, 9/11/01 in another; 3.30 p.m. in one place, 15:30 in another); careless variation in units (inches in one place and centimetres in another). The book you are now reading will alert you to these and similar matters to ensure that your message is free of such distractions and that it carries itself with a dash of style: your readers will stay focused on the substance of your message, but will also sense the professional touch in the way it is presented.

Why you should use this handbook

The handbook is a handy reference whenever you find yourself looking for answers to questions such as these, which arise routinely in communicating technical information formally.

- What should a list such as this use to mark off items: bullet points, numbers, or letters?
- Where do you cite the source of unpublished data: within the document or at the end, under references?
- Which font makes it easier to tell apart such similar-looking pairs of characters as a zero (0) and the letter 'o', the numeral one (1) and the letter 'l' ('ell')?
- When should you distribute handouts, before the presentation or after?
- How are web pages cited when they are referred to in a document?

> Behind the work of the technical editors lies a powerful tool called house style. ⋯ Some of the principles of house style are standards of good writing; some can be robustly defended—such as our eschewing of most abbreviations in a journal that is read by an enormous variety of readers; and others are admittedly arbitrary. But even the arbitrary ones can be justified on the grounds that we need to make a decision and stick to it: our readers probably wouldn't thank us for changes in spellings, capitalisation, and units of measurement between one article and the next.
>
> Cooter M. 1999. Putting on the style [editorial]. *British Medical Journal* **319**: 1592.

> As to the form May 19, 1862, Sir James Murray said, 'This is not logical: 19 May 1862 is. Begin at day, ascend to month, ascend to year; not begin at month, descend to day, then ascend to year.'
>
> Hart H. 1983. *Hart's Rules for Compositors and Readers at the University Press*, Oxford, 39th edn, p. 18. Oxford, UK: Oxford University Press. 182 pp.

> Address   www.tiresias.org/guidelines/fonts.htm
>
> This website is an information resource for professionals who work in the field of visual disabilities. The site has evolved from work carried out by Dr Janet Silver of Moorfields Eye Hospital, London and Dr John Gill of the Royal National Institute of the Blind. ⋯
>
> In many sans serif typefaces the lower case is visually similar to the capital. For instance, Charles III Ill is more difficult to read in Arial than in Tiresias.
>
> Increasingly password and email addresses use both letters and numbers. For such applications it is essential to use a typeface which clearly differentiates the numeral 1 and lower case l.

```
1  l  I    Arial
1  l  I    Times New Roman
1  l  I    Verdana
```

Numeral one, lower-case 'l', and capital 'I' in three typefaces

The minutiae of style

The handbook grew out of queries posed by the staff of a research institute – TERI or The Energy and Resources Institute, in New Delhi, India – over a decade during the course of publishing formal technical communications in a wide range of subjects. In some ways, it is a compilation of FAQs (frequently asked questions). If nothing else, referring to it will save a great deal of your time as well as that of your readers. The advice presented here will also directly help you to make a more favourable impression on colleagues, clients, funding agencies, reviewers, employers, and all those who judge you, consciously or unconsciously, by how you present what you know. If you are a researcher or an academician, this handbook will help you to get your research papers reviewed more favourably and published faster once they are accepted.

What is style and why it matters

In communicating technical information, style settles a number of issues, trivial individually but significant collectively, that influence the overall impact of the message. Style also makes information more precise and more easily accessible.

The minutiae of style are hallmarks of precise communication. Take the format for dates, for instance: 6/1/2003 can mean either the 6th of January or the 1st of June of the year 2003. This handbook, therefore, recommends the format that gives the date as 6 January 2003 or 1 June 2003: the day first and as a *cardinal* number (not as an *ordinal* number as in 1st or 1st) without a leading zero (6 and not 06); the month spelt out in full (January and not Jan.); and the year expressed in all the four digits (2003 and not '03).

E-mail addresses are another example. Consider the address <I.lo10@hotmail.com>: it is essential to distinguish clearly between the numeral '1' and the letters 'l' and 'I' and to ensure that the lower-case 'o' is not mistaken for the numeral 'o' — fonts such as Times New Roman or Arial will not do the job effectively. The handbook therefore recommends Verdana. On similar grounds, it is always better to spell out litre or litres

Chapter 1 Style for effective communication

> **Quote**
>
> Address: http://bmj.com/advice/stylebook/lbook.shtml
>
> bmj.com — From the British Medical Journal web site
>
> **Full contents**
> **Article submission**
> **BMJ contact details**
> **BMJ ethics committee**
> **BMJ peer review process**
> **BMJ sections**
> **BMJ style:**
>   Basics
>   Style book
>   making articles more
>
> **BMJ house style**
>
> **The Essentials**
>
> Please write in a clear, direct, and active style.
> The BMJ is an international journal, and many readers do not have English as their
>
> Our preferred dictionaries are
>
> - Chambers 21st Century Dictionary for general usage
> - Dorlands for medical terms.
>
> If there's going to be confusion between the number 1 and the letter l, spell out litre (don't use L)

Example

✗ Part II   ✓ Part 2

✗	✓
i	1
ii	2
iii	3
iv	4
v	5

Prefer arabic numerals to roman numerals.

Example

✗ Table 1 Emissions of air pollutants attributed to the transport sector

✓ Table 1 Emissions of air pollutants attributed to the transport sector

Set table titles in normal font; do not make them bold.

Resources

A selection of style guides

in full instead of using the standard symbol (a lower-case 'l') or using the capital form (L), a standard practice in USA and Canada. Style affects the usability of documents. For instance, what is the point of projecting an overhead transparency if it is illegible? Why provide headings and subheadings if the design fails to distinguish between them clearly? Why use a light colour for the cover of a report if it is easily soiled? Why use subtle shades of grey, which do not show up well if photocopied? Such considerations govern many of the decisions about style. For instance, arabic numerals (1, 2, 3, 4, etc.) are recommended instead of roman numerals (i, ii, iii, iv, etc.) because arabic numerals are compact and familiar: for numbers up to ten, arabic numerals are read in only half the time it takes to read roman numerals; for larger numbers, arabic numerals are taken in even faster, in just one-fifth of the time (Perry 1952). And the reason for suggesting that only the word 'Table' and the number that follows it should appear in bold, instead of setting everything in bold – including the title of the table – is to make the number stand out from the surrounding text: a table is mentioned in text by its number, and it is the number that readers look for as they scan the document in search of that table.

Sources of advice and information

For most part, the style described in this handbook follows the best traditions of such renowned scholarly publishers as Oxford University Press and Cambridge University Press. In matters of spelling, for example, the handbook follows the British practice (hence analyse and not analyze). However, no single style guide can answer every query, and the author has searched far and wide for good advice, including instructions to authors of many respected journals, web pages of several American university presses, style guides of the World Bank and the World Resources Institute, relevant journals such as the *Journal of Scholarly Publishing* and *Information Design Journal*,

Resources

A selection of books and periodicals

Resource

Address: www.electriceditors.net/edline/index.htm

EDline — for editorial discussions

- What is EDline?
- Subscriptions
- Posting messages to EDline

Quote

After 'Dear X', put a comma or nothing at all. ··· (In American English, a comma is preferred in personal letters, and a colon (:) in business letters.)
    Swan M. 1995. *Practical English Usage*, 2nd edn, p. 308. Oxford, UK: Oxford University Press. 658 pp.

newsletters and bulletins of such professional organizations as the Council of Science Editors and the European Association of Science Editors, and several printers, designers, and editors within and outside India. Several 'lists' (discussion groups) on the Internet proved to be particularly useful sources of specific and up-to-date advice. Many researchers, editors, and designers have made valuable contributions to developing the style, often by pointing out the difficulties and pitfalls in implementing some of the recommendations (which were then changed accordingly and are included in this handbook).

Developing a distinctive style

Distinctive appearance is a mark of style: it not only sets the products of one publisher apart from those of another but also identifies the publisher. Logos, colours, and fonts are some of the more obvious devices used to establish a style but a publisher's style is a more subtle matter. Many seemingly arbitrary points of style are in fact a publisher's way of giving individual identity to his or her products. As *The World Bank Publications Style Manual* puts it in its opening sentence, 'A style manual codifies the arbitrary, the conventional, and the trivial' (World Bank 1991, p. 1). For every style ruling that can be defended on grounds of logic, usability, or authority, there are dozens that have no more solid basis than tradition, taste, or judgement. And these are just the kind that go on to make a unique style.

Take a trivial matter: would you add a comma after the salutation when writing a letter? A colon perhaps? Nothing? The traditional British practice is to use a comma whereas in most American business correspondence you would find a colon. The more modern style uses neither. By itself, any of the alternatives is perfectly acceptable so long as it is used consistently—what you choose marks your style. Consider the manner of expressing physical quantities, to take a more scientific example. To say that one cubic metre of air contained 3 milligrams of fine dust, you could use two types of notation,

✗ The basic requirement in positron emission tomography (PET) is for either oxygen or glucose to be labelled so that it can be easily tracked.

✓ The basic requirement in PET (positron emission tomography) is for either oxygen or glucose to be labelled so that it can be easily tracked.

Give the shorter version first, followed by the spelt-out version within brackets.

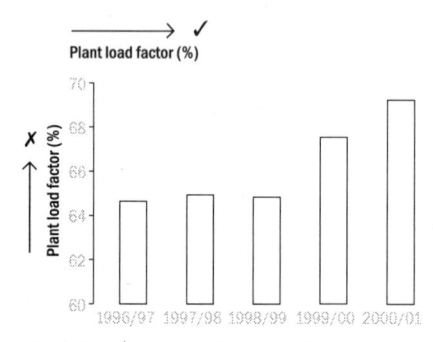

Place the label for the vertical axis at the top, running from left to right.

> An example is the treatment of titles such as Mr and Mrs: it is widely accepted that they do not take full points, and even though some printers advocated this practice in the late 19th century, it was not until 1978 that it was accepted in Hart's *Rules*.
> Walker S. 1993. Happy birthday Hart's *Rules*.
> *Information Design Journal* 7: 177–178

Mister	Mr
Doctor	Dr
Private	Pvt
Limited	Ltd
Professor	Prof

Skip the full stop after *contractions* (when first and last letters of shorter and longer versions are the same).

namely the slash or a negative exponent: you could write 3 mg/m³ or 3 mg m⁻³ or 3 mg·m⁻³ (with a space or a raised dot) and be equally correct—again, your choice adds to the style. Here is a miscellany of such arbitrary choices recommended in this handbook.

- In explaining abbreviations, give the shorter version first, followed by its explanation within parentheses, instead of the other way around.
- Prefer left justification, which gives a zigzag right-hand margin but ensures uniform spacing between words, to full justification, which gives a straight right-hand edge but awkward or uneven spacing between words.
- Use squares or triangles as bullet points instead of circles.
- In graphs, place the label for the vertical axis at the top, running from left to right like normal text, instead of placing it sideways and to the left of the axis.
- Avoid vertical or horizontal lines (rules) to separate columns or rows within a table.
- Differentiate between abbreviations and contractions by adding a full stop after abbreviations but dropping it after contractions, as in Pvt. Ltd for private limited (plc in Britain), where the first item is an abbreviation and the second is a contraction.

The essentials of style

The essence of style, distilled from a large collection of specific style recommendations, is the following representative list of preferences.

> Keep in mind what the readers would find helpful instead of doing what is easiest for you

Technical writing is essentially to inform: you, as a writer, already know—the question is, How well do you communicate what you know to others? To quote from a prospectus prepared by the Document Design Center in Washington, DC, 'Informative documents should anticipate and answer the

| Address | http://tejas.serc.iisc.ernet.in/currsci/dec252002/1432.pdf | Quote |

It is often taken for granted that a person reading a scientific communication should know the expansions for all acronyms used, which, however, is not true. A simple test was given by me to a group of postgraduate biology students, where I had asked them to write the expansion for DNA. Although all of them knew about DNA, surprisingly only 10% of the students correctly wrote the expansion.

Krishnamurthy K V. 2002. The menace of acronyms. *Current Science* **83**: 1432–1433

| Address | www.lighthouse.org/BigType/boomers.htm | Quote |

Big Type is Best for Aging Baby Boomers:
A Case for Universal Graphic Design
Baby boomers, take heed: your vision is diminishing... rapidly.

LIGHTHOUSE INTERNATIONAL
HOPE WHEN VISION FAILS

Recognizing the growing need of this boomer population, mainstream publications like *Reader's Digest* and *The New York Times* are printing large type editions—and have turned to Lighthouse International for guidance.

| Address | http://psychology.wichita.edu/surl/usabilitynews/3W/fontSR.htm | Quote |

Usability News 3.1 2001
SURL Home > Usability News
Determining the Best Online Font for Older Adults

Several observations can be made from these findings. First, 14-point fonts were found to be more legible, promote faster reading, and were preferred to the 12-point fonts. ··· Thus, in light of these results, it is recommended to use 14-point sized fonts for presenting online text to older readers.

questions that the reader might have, they should help the reader find specific information in the document, and they should enable the reader to take appropriate action' (Felker, Redish, and Peterson 1985, p. 53). Every decision, small or large, that you take as a writer should reflect concern for the reader. For example, you may wish to organize the topic of air pollution by individual pollutant (carbon monoxide, oxides of nitrogen, suspended particulate matter) whereas your readers may prefer arrangement by source (motor cars, thermal power stations, factories).

Use abbreviations sparingly

A liberal sprinkling of abbreviations not only makes a page look spotty but, and more important, discourages all readers other than those who are familiar with the shorthand. As the World Bank's style manual puts it (World Bank 1991, p. 12), 'The confusion from using obscure abbreviations, even if they are defined once, is not worth the space saved.' Abbreviations can often mislead: PIN stands for postal index number (a post code) in India but denotes personal identification number in Europe.

Choose larger fonts

Most of your readers are professionals with at least some work experience, and therefore they are likely to be in their thirties or older and would prefer a comfortable font for sustained reading. Times New Roman (including its related versions) is too small at 10 points and packs far too many letters into each line of text when set in a single column. Times New Roman at 12 points is large but not black enough to ensure good contrast both while reading and photocopying.

Larger fonts are essential for text meant to be read off a screen. The coarse resolution (96 pixels per inch in Windows) of computer monitors makes it difficult for smaller fonts (12 points or smaller) to be displayed legibly.

Capitalisation This is the source of great tribulation. Please adhere to the following guidance. Too many capital letters are ugly. Capitals interrupt the passage of the eye along a line. They are often unnecessary, especially with non-proper nouns such as government or ministry. Struggle to avoid them unless to do so looks absurd.

> The Times. 1992. *The Times Guide to English Style and Usage*, p. 33. London: Times Books. 190 pp.

Address www.economist.com/research/styleGuide/

Capitals
A balance has to be struck between so many capitals that the eyes dance and so few that the reader is diverted more by our style than by our substance. ··· More exact rules are laid out below. Even these, however, leave some decisions to individual judgment. If in doubt use lower case unless it looks absurd.

Pearsall J (ed.). 1998. *The New Oxford Dictionary of English*. Oxford, UK: Clarendon Press. 2152 pp.

Follow the *New Oxford Dictionary of English* in matters of spelling.

Prefer small letters to capital letters; use capitals only when you must

Generally, capitals go with particular entities or specified members of a class whereas small letters go with unspecified members. In the 'Government of Punjab', for instance, the 'G' is capitalized because one particular government is being referred to whereas in 'state governments should enact specific legislation', the 'g' is lower-case because no particular state government is mentioned.

Follow the *New Oxford Dictionary of English* in matters of spelling

Because British spellings (colour instead of color, centre instead of center) are far more commonly used in India than American spellings, use British spellings consistently. The choice is essentially pragmatic because typesetters, proofreaders, and editors are, to quote the *Chicago Manual of Style*, 'far more likely to catch inconsistencies when they are departures from normal ··· spellings than when they are departures from less familiar ··· forms' (University of Chicago Press 1993, p. 195). The matter of the appropriate authority for spellings is dealt with in greater detail in Annexe B.

References

Felker D B, Redish J C, and Peterson J. 1985
Training authors of informative documents, pp. 43–61
in *Designing Usable Texts*, edited by T M Duffy and R Waller
Orlando, Florida, USA: Academic Press. 423 pp.

Perry D K. 1952
Speed and accuracy of reading Arabic and Roman numerals
Journal of Applied Psychology **36**: 346–347

University of Chicago Press. 1993
***The Chicago Manual of Style**: the essential guide for writers, editors, and publishers*, 14th edn
Chicago, Illinois, USA: University of Chicago Press. 921 pp.

World Bank. 1991
The World Bank Publications Style Manual
Washington, DC: The World Bank. 50 pp.

Chapter **1** Style for effective communication

Chapter 2 at a glance

Functions of headings
The text of headings
The number of levels of headings
A hierarchy of headings
Space above and below headings
Capitals and punctuation marks in headings
Headings that span more than one line
Headings and indents
Appropriate levels of headings
Numbered headings
Effective headings: some reminders
References

▶ 2 Heads, you win; text, I lose
signposting documents with headings

A fast-paced novel is something you would love to read at one sitting but technical documents are seldom – if at all – read from cover to cover in one go. Technical documents are essentially reference documents, to be dipped into for information: sometimes in large doses, sometimes in spoonfuls. This is apparent in the way most readers approach the task of reading any non-fiction: they pick up a document and leaf through it casually, turning pages at random and pausing to read a few lines here and there or to look at a graph or a table; some choose to study the table of contents to see what the document is all about; in the case of reports, many expect a summary. Also, readers often return to a document, looking for something they have read before. Therefore, it is essential to structure a document to match this pattern of use and it is the job of headings to make that structure apparent. Williams (1990) maintains that writers use headings 'to diagnose potential problems with the perceived structure of a document' and Hartley and Trueman (1985) present experimental evidence to show that headings help the 'recall, search and retrieval of information'.

To design an effective hierarchy of headings, you need to keep in mind a number of issues including the following, which are further discussed in this chapter.

▹ How many levels of headings – major headings, subheadings, sub-subheadings, minor headings, and so on – should a document use?
▹ What are the ways to signal a heading's position in a hierarchy?
▹ Should headings be numbered?
▹ How should long headings be handled?
▹ Do headings take a full stop when text follows them on the same line?

Introduction
How much is the world warming?
Is the recent warming unusual?
How rapidly did climate change in the distant past?
How have precipitation and atmospheric moisture changed?
Are the atmospheric/oceanic circulations changing?
Has climate variability, or have climate extremes, changed?
Are the observed trends internally consistent?
References

Major headings from Chapter 2 of *Climate Change 2001: the Scientific Basis, Contribution of Working Group 1 to the Third Assessment Report of the Intergovernmental Panel on Climate Change*

Structurally similar headings

Address	www.useit.com/alertbox/980906.html

Microcontent: how to write headlines, page titles, and subject lines
Microcontent needs to be pearls of clarity: you get 40–60 characters to explain your macrocontent. Unless the title or subject make it absolutely clear what the page or email is about, users will never open it.
  Nielsen J. 1998. Microcontent: how to write headlines, page titles, and subject lines

The first sentence of text following a subhead should not refer syntactically to the subhead; words should be repeated where necessary.
  University of Chicago Press. 2003. *The Chicago Manual of Style*, 15th edn, p. 26 [section 1.78]. Chicago, Illinois, USA: University of Chicago Press. 956 pp.

Functions of headings

Headings make information more easily accessible and documents more usable because they

- facilitate scanning and offer a quick overview of the document
- break up large blocks of text, which makes text not only more accessible but also less daunting in appearance
- tell readers more about the scope of the document by showing how much space is devoted to each section
- highlight how information is organized within a document and thus help recall
- help readers find what they are looking for more quickly, especially in documents that lack an index
- build a visual image of the contents, which facilitates locating information in the second and subsequent readings.

The text of headings

Word the headings carefully—they have a much larger readership than body text does. Try to impose a similar grammatical structure for all the headings that are at the same level (all chapters in a book, all major headings in a chapter, all subheadings in a section, and so on). They can all be questions or instructions or noun phrases or whatever; what is important is that they all share the same structure.

Treat a heading and the text that follows it as independent entities. For instance, if the heading is 'Enzyme', do not begin the text with 'This is a substance produced by living cells that catalyses specific biochemical reactions'. In other words, do not begin the text with a pronoun that has as its antecedent a noun mentioned in the heading even when the text follows the heading on the same line.

The number of levels of headings

Nearly all the decisions that you need to make if the structure of your document is to be apparent to readers will be influenced by the number of different levels of headings you

In running text a reader finds a great variety of headings confusing rather than helpful; and it is difficult for the designer to specify more than three kinds of heading that will be sufficiently distinct from one another and from table headings, running heads, etc.
    Butcher J. 1992. *Copy-editing: the Cambridge handbook for editors, authors and publishers*, p. 207. Cambridge, UK: Cambridge University Press. 471 pp.

Quote

Typographically speaking, the distinctions among subheads needn't be dramatic, just self-evident. There's no formula that defines how much bigger a level-A subhead should be than a level-B, or a level-B subhead than a level-C.
    Felici J. 2003. *The Complete Manual of Typography: a guide to setting perfect type*, p. 218. Berkeley, California, USA: Peachpit Press. 361 pp.

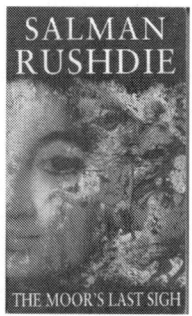

Quote

Example

Celebrity authors: 'who' is more important than 'what'

have used—try and keep that number to three (major headings, subheadings, and minor headings, or A-level, B-level, and C-level). In exceptional cases, you may add another level (D-level). Consider reorganizing the document into parts or volumes if you find that even four levels are inadequate. This upper limit of four levels may sound arbitrary but remember that headings are signposts: they are meant to guide the readers through a document, not lose them in a maze.

A hierarchy of headings

Most technical documents are complex enough to require not just some headings but a proper scheme made up of different levels of headings: major headings, subheadings, minor headings, and so on. Just as the military insignia makes it easy to identify rank – two stripes for a corporal and three for a sergeant – appropriately designed headings establish a hierarchy. A simple way to judge this is to ask someone who is unfamiliar with the subject to construct an outline of headings for a section of a document merely by looking at the way the headings are formatted; if the headings are styled appropriately, it should be easy enough to draw up such an outline.

The hierarchy of headings is established by a combination of choices. For instance, we can differentiate between two levels by making one larger than the other, or by making one bold, or by using different fonts, or by a combination of these options. No matter what combination we choose, the objective is to signal the level of importance of each type of heading clearly. The title of the document is usually the most important item and is made very prominent. With best-selling authors, you will observe that it is the other way around: the fact that it is an Agatha Christie novel is more important than its title. If we consider a chapter as a unit, then the chapter title should be the most prominent item in that unit, followed by major headings, which are less prominent than the title but more prominent than subheadings. Subheadings, in turn, are more prominent than minor headings, and so on down the line until

2 ▶ Heads, you win; text, I lose

Signposting documents with headings

Example

> A fast-paced novel is something you would love to read at one sitting but technical documents are seldom – if at all – read from cover to cover in one go. Technical documents are essentially reference documents, to be dipped into for information: sometimes in large doses, sometimes in spoonfuls.

A prominently displayed chapter title

The way people understand graphic structure

Relative size Type that is bigger or bolder is seen as more important ⋯
Similarity Things that look alike are seen as belonging to the same category ⋯
Relative proximity Things that are close together are seen as related.
Enclosure Things that are enclosed in the same space are seen as related.
Alignment Things that line up with one another are seen as related.
  Waller R. 1991. *Designing Forms and Catalogues*, p. 12–13. Redhill, Surrey, UK: Monotype Corporation. 32 pp. [Monotype Desktop Solutions series, edited by Andrew Boag]

Quote

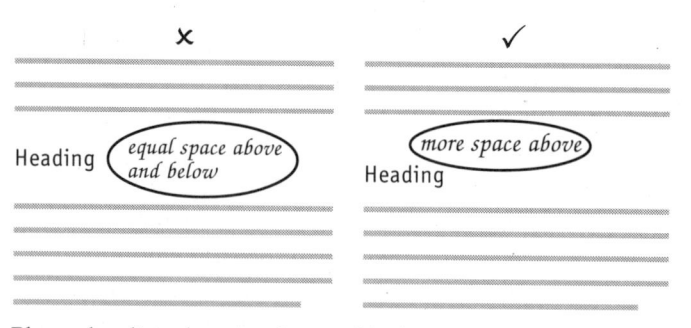

✗   ✓

Heading (*equal space above and below*)

(*more space above*) Heading

Example

Place a heading closer to the text block it refers to; never suspend a heading exactly midway between two blocks of text.

we reach continuous text, which is not highlighted in any way at all. The logic is that as we move up the ladder, the levels begin to look more and more different from plain text. Waller (1991), in his useful booklet titled *Designing Forms and Catalogues*, offers the following principles that underpin effective page layouts.

- Larger or darker type is seen as more important than smaller or lighter type.
- Headings that are formatted alike are seen as belonging to the same category.
- Blocks of text (or other matter) enclosed in the same space, set close together, or aligned with each other are seen as related.

The format used in this handbook illustrates the concept: the font used for the text is 10.8-point Hoefler Text Roman whereas chapter titles are set in 20-point Officina Sans Bold. This makes a chapter title different from the text in every way: it is larger (20 points versus 10.8 points), darker (bold versus normal), and set in an altogether different typeface (Officina Sans versus Hoefler). Moreover, the chapter title is prominent because it is

- always placed at the top of a page;
- aligned to the right instead of to the left;
- separated from the rest of the text with a horizontal line running the entire width of the page; and
- paired with a prominently displayed chapter number.

Space above and below headings

Always ensure that a heading is closer to the text block that follows it than the block of text that comes before. In other words, the space above a heading should always be greater than that below the heading so that, visually, the bond between the heading and the text is clear. Never suspend a heading exactly midway between two blocks of text so that it fails to show its affinity.

It follows, therefore, that every heading should be seen along with at least a part of the text to which it relates: a

> Words are perceived by their specific word-shape outline, which is unique for lower-case words. Once the outline of the words has been perceived and stored in memory, future recognition or recall of the word takes place without letter-by-letter deciphering. Words set in all caps, however, do not provide specific word-shape outlines since they produce an oblong, uniform word shape. ··· Words set in all caps use up to 30% more space than words set in lower-case, which leads to an increase in time-consuming eye fixations; 4.74 words per second, one study showed, can be read in all-caps type, and 5.38 words can be read in lower-case type.
>
> Text set in all caps retards reading speed by about 13%, due to an increase in fixation time, and results in a corresponding decrease in the number of words perceived per fixation.
>
> Rehe R F. 2000. *Legibility,* in *Graphic Design and Printing: explorations of an uneasy relationship,* pp. 96–109, edited by G Swanson. New York: Allworth Press. 221 pp.

✗ Abatement Costs of Health Impacts of Polluted Water

✓ Abatement costs of health impacts of polluted water

Avoid starting every word in a heading with a capital letter.

Soil degradation Soil degradation is widespread in India (57% of the total land area in 1998).

Separate run-on headings from the following text with space; do not end such headings with a full stop or a colon.

> Address http://ascilite.org.au/ajet/ajet7/priestly.html
>
> The conclusion then by researchers who are concerned with reading for understanding and long term comprehension is do not use capital letters for emphasis.
>
> Priestly W. 1991. Instructional typographies using desktop publishing techniques to produce effective learning and training materials. *Australian Journal of Educational Technology* 7: 153–163

heading that falls at the end of a page fails on this count, and should be avoided. Make sure that at least two full lines of text follow a heading. If this is not possible, it is better to leave a few lines blank at the end of a page and begin the next page with the heading.

The only exception to this rule is when one heading follows another without any intervening text. In that case, you may place the lower of the two headings with equal space above and below; the way in which headings are formatted makes it clear that one is subordinate to the other. The higher of the two headings follows the norm, with more space above (separating it from the text that comes before) and less space below (showing its closer affinity to the heading below).

Capitals and punctuation marks in headings

Though headings are different from text in terms of appearance, they should follow the same conventions of capitalization and punctuation as those that govern plain text.

Do not set any heading entirely in capital letters. Using capital letters in this manner not only wastes space but also masks the characteristic shapes of individual words, making them hard to read. It is particularly difficult to spot errors of spelling in any text set entirely in capitals. Besides, some information may be lost when text is set entirely in capitals: for instance, Macmillan, the publishers, always spell their name *without* capitalizing the second M, a distinction that is lost if the word is set as MACMILLAN.

Avoid starting every word in a heading with a capital letter, a style that has been said to cause 'visual hiccups' (Lichty 1989). Keep the capitals only for proper nouns.

For headings that have one or more lines to themselves (the text that follows a heading starts on a new line), do not use any closing punctuation mark such as a colon or a dash or a full stop—it serves no useful purpose. Headings may end with a question mark or an exclamation mark should the sense require one.

Chapter **2** Heads, you win; text, I lose

> ··· since difficulties of reading aloud are eased by breaking prose at points that make sense rather than at the end of a line, it was not implausible that difficulties in understanding could be eased using the same strategy.
>
> Wainer H. 1997. *Visual Revelations: graphical tales of fate and deception from Napoleon Bonaparte to Ross Perot*, p. 152. New York: Copernicus (Springer-Verlag). 180 pp.

> Using an indent for the first line of each paragraph, as opposed to inter-paragraph spacing, provides visual separation without too much interruption ··· When headings are used with this paragraphing format, the first line of text following the heading should not be indented. ··· This blocking of first paragraphs provides a square corner, which looks 'cleaner' than an indent would in this position.
>
> [Revised by] Snooks & Co. 2002. *Style Manual for Authors, Editors and Printers*, 6th edn, p. 336. Canberra: John Wiley & Sons Australia. 550 pp.

Avoid ending a heading, especially a chapter title, with a footnote- or endnote-marker.

Separate a heading from the text that follows it on the same line with a fixed amount of space and only with space: do not close the heading with a colon; do not close it with a full stop either unless the heading takes the form of a sentence.

Headings that span more than one line

Technical documents often have long titles and headings. Sometimes, such headings run into two lines. It then becomes important to control the line-breaks consciously. Always break such headings by sense; in other words, choose a logical break. In the following examples, the pipe sign (|) marks a logical break: 'Basic approach of developing countries to the | negotiations for a climate change convention' or 'Legal and institutional issues arising out of the | proposed Framework Convention on Climate Change'. If a title consists of a title and subtitle, keep the title on one line and the subtitle on the next line if space allows it. (See the title of this chapter as an example.)

A startling violation of this principle is seen quite close to the TERI block in New Delhi. A notice, painted in bright red and large letters, appears near Gate 3. It says: Visitors to India | Habitat Centre | Please park inside. The first reaction to the notice with these line-breaks is that it is meant for visitors to India; only on second reading does it strike readers that the notice is meant for visitors to the India Habitat Centre (Visitors to | India Habitat Centre | Please park inside).

Headings and indents

The first line after a heading is set flush with the left margin but lines that begin the second and subsequent paragraphs are indented normally. This convention works well most of the time but comes under strain when the heading is immediately followed by a lower-level heading set indented as a matter of style. In such cases, the scheme of headings needs to be altered

> **Address** www.unb.ca/extend/wss/apa5.htm
>
> QuickNotes on APA Format
> APA (American Psychological Association) style guide offers 'five possible formatting arrangements according to the number of levels of subordination. Although each level is numbered, the *specific levels used are not necessarily consecutive*.' [emphasis added]

Quote

1 Specifications for a 2-column setting

1.1 Column width and inter-column spacing

1.2 Font and line spacing

1.2.1 Font

1.2.2 Line spacing

2 Specifications for a multicolumn setting

2.1 Number of columns

Example

Assign a separate column for the numbers when using numbered headings. Align the numbers to the right.

such that the higher-level headings are also indented, an alternative adopted in this handbook.

Appropriate levels of headings

Assigning correct levels to headings is not something that can be done mechanically because different chapters within a single document may have been structured differently. A long chapter, covering a topic exhaustively, may require several levels of headings whereas a short chapter, giving only a concise account of a topic, may use just one level of headings. Now, applying the style mechanically would mean treating all of them as though they were major (or A-level) headings, making them so prominent as to be overwhelming. The effect is worse when blocks of text under each of them are small and several headings fall on a single page or within a page-spread, making the pages look blotchy. In such a situation, use your judgement. As the World Bank's guidelines[a] put it, 'If only two subhead levels are needed, use levels A and B. If only one is needed, use level B.'

Numbered headings

Many official documents prefer a numerical system to a typographic system for indicating the levels of headings. Under the numerical system, all major headings are numbered 1, 2, 3, and so on; all subheadings under Heading 1 are numbered 1.1, 1.2, 1.3, etc. whereas all those under Heading 2 are numbered 2.1, 2.2, 2.3, etc. Minor headings are designated 1.1.1, 1.1.2, 1.1.3, etc. Some documents use the zero as well, numbering the major headings 0, 1, 2, etc. and the subheadings 1.0, 1.1, 1.2, etc.

The numerical system makes it easy to refer precisely to any portion of the document. You may consider using such a system if you think that the document will be extensively referred to and commented upon, especially if you are to revise the document after such feedback. The system is also handy for

[a] *Communications and Style Guide*: guidelines for preparing internal documents, June 1992 (unpublished)

Chapter **2** Heads, you win; text, I lose

> **Address** www.raycomm.com/techwhirl/archives/0211/techwhirl-0211-01061.html
>
> [whether to assign numbers to headings] Depends on the document and the audience. If the numbers are largely arbitrary, and the document only used sporadically, probably not very useful.
> However, nuclear propulsion plant manuals in the Navy are heavily numbered, and if you refer to Operating Instruction 9.3.7.2, engineering personnel will at least know what the 9.3 means (and may recognize the whole thing, if it is a frequently used procedure). If I remember right, the first number identified a system, the second the type of procedure (startup, normal, abnormal, shutdown, etc).
>
> Holmes G. 2002. Message dated 21 November 2002 posted to TECHWR-L ['tech-whirl' is an Internet-based community and resource for technical communicators worldwide.]

> **Address** www.raycomm.com/techwhirl/archives/9507/techwhirl-9507-00584.html
>
> ··· numbered headers are ··· certainly are a more succinct method for accurately referring a reader to another location. The reader immediately knows whether to page forward or backward ··· numbered headers eliminate the need to add little helping comments like 'later in this chapter' ···
> Formatting numbered headers is also a problem, since the text of the header may end up right of the center of the page! My preference is to run the number to the left of the left-handed text margin, in a negative relationship to the margin setting. But then you need large margins and a large gutter.
>
> Freiman F. 1995. Message dated 21 November 2002 posted to TECHWR-L

cross-references within the document when one or more of its sections are frequently referred to in other sections. Yet another point in favour of the system is that a document can be indexed even before the final pagination so long as the index refers not to page numbers but to section numbers. However, these are merely superficial conveniences; as an aid to comprehension, Waller (1980) calls numbered headings cryptic, insincere, and officious: cryptic, in that the notation is rarely explained; insincere, in that 'they purport to aid the reader while in fact they often mislead' (they present text as discrete blocks of text, making its readers miss the wood for the trees); and officious, in that they bestow on the text a 'phoney air of authority'.

If you decide to use the numerical system, keep typographic formatting to the minimum because the decimal numbering itself is a cue to the level of any heading. Usually, it is enough to simply set all the major headings in bold, with one blank line above, without changing any other attribute of the font. As far as possible, use a 2-column format, with a narrow left-hand column only for the numbers and a broad right-hand column for the text and use the same font throughout the text. Align the numbers *to the right* so that the space between a number and the corresponding heading is always the same. The lines of text are shorter than those set with a single-column format, so you can set them closer. In particular, do not use any special formatting for the numbers.

Headings within tables (both column heads and row heads) are covered in Chapter 6, which deals with tabular matter.

Effective headings: some reminders

▸ Consider the size of the page and the amount of text that follows a heading in deciding how large the heading should be. For an A4-size paper (210 mm by 297 mm), 24 points is probably the upper limit for the title of a paper or a chapter; 18 points should work well enough. For main headings within the body of a document, 14 points is large enough. If

> Underlining as a method of emphasizing a word or phrase in a displayed setting is a crude relic of Victorian typography. Emphasis can, and should, be achieved in other ways, for example by the judicious use of capitals, or bold capitals, or by the use of roman or italic bold or extra heavy types in upper- and lower-case.
>
> Dowding G. 1995. *Finer Points in the Spacing and Arrangement of Type*, 3rd rev. edn, pp. 77–78. Vancouver, Canada: Hartley & Marks. 90 pp.

Headings with a 'negative indent'   Headings in a separate column

> It should be a part of your routine to periodically read your headings in isolation, without the distractions of your text. Focusing on the headings in isolation makes it much easier for you to judge how well you have organized your text, whether you have divided it into manageable blocks, whether you have in fact ordered your material logically, and whether you have overlooked or duplicated some detail. It also helps you proofread your headings – remember that when your document is printed the headings will stand out very clearly (that's the idea after all) and simple spelling errors will cause you major embarrassment.
>
> Carol Miller
> Publications unit, Australian Sports Commission
> [e-mail message dated 25 Feb. 2000]

headings apply to short blocks of text, make the headings less obtrusive.
- Avoid using bold or italics for long headings (about 25 characters, including spaces between words).
- Use white space, weight, and ornaments sparingly. Headings surrounded by ample blank space, headings set in bold, and headings used in combination with such graphic devices as lines and icons are very prominent; reserve such treatment for major headings alone.
- Do not underline; it was common in the days of the manual typewriter but is now commonly associated with links in hypertext.
- Pull headings into the left margin or push them away from it: headings that are out of alignment with text, either because they are indented (as in this handbook) or extend into the margins (commonly known as a negative indent) are distinct enough to be noticed while scanning but are not so prominent as to be overpowering. Many textbooks and manuals place headings in a separate column altogether.

References

Hartley J and Trueman M. 1985
A research strategy for text designers: the role of headings
Instructional Science **14**: 99–155

Lichty T. 1989
Design Principles for Desktop Publishers, p. 77
Glenview, Illinois, USA: Scott, Foresman and Co. 201 pp.

Waller R. 1980
3.2 Notes on transforming nos 4 and 5
in *The Psychology of Written Communication: selected readings*, pp. 145–159, edited by J Hartley
London: Kogan Page and New York: Nichols Publishing. 301 pp.

Waller R. 1991
Designing Forms and Catalogues
Redhill, Surrey, UK: Monotype Corporation. 32 pp.
[Monotype Desktop Solutions series, edited by Andrew Boag]

Williams J M. 1990
Style: toward clarity and grace
Chicago, Illinois, USA: University of Chicago Press. 208 pp.

Chapter 3 at a glance

Lists embedded within running text
Keeping listed items parallel
Choice of item markers
Formatting of the item markers
Formatting a nested list
Punctuation in lists
Space between a list and surrounding text
The length of a list
Typographic refinements
References

Make a list
formatting and punctuating items in a series

Lists are common in technical writing because they display information concisely yet prominently. 'Bulleted' text is particularly useful for those who are searching for information in text they have already read because 'bulleting' helps them find that information faster: '··· the richer formatting aids readers in organising and memorising document information rather than in navigating through the document on first encounter' (Human Communication Research Centre 1999). Such lists are almost always preferred to continuous text in presentations (PowerPoint files, overhead transparencies, 35-mm slides, and so on).

Presenting information in list form raises several queries, and this chapter attempts to answer most of them.
- How to choose between different 'item markers' (bullet points, numbers, letters, and so on)
- How to handle 'nested' lists (lists within lists)
- How to punctuate a list
- Whether each item in a list should begin with a capital letter
- Whether a list should be separated from surrounding text with extra space

Lists embedded within running text

Lists are either embedded ('run on') or 'displayed'. A run-on list takes the form of a continuous stream of text in which the items are listed one after the other, usually separated with commas or semicolons, without any conspicuous break—each new item *does not* begin on a fresh line; also, the entire list is ordinarily part of a single sentence. A displayed list, on the other hand, always assigns a fresh line to each item, marks each item with a marker, and may run to more than one sentence. Sometimes, one or more items in a list may themselves run to more than one sentence (in which case the list is punctuated accordingly).

Address http://stipo.larc.nasa.gov/sp7084/sp7084.pdf

Because of its strong separating function, an introductory colon should generally be used only after a complete sentence. In particular, do not use a colon between a verb or preposition and its direct object:
  Wrong The components of the rack-mounted electronics are: power supplies, the gimbal controller, ···
  Correct The components of the rack-mounted electronics are power supplies, the gimbal controller, ···
  There is a trend toward using a colon after a verb preceding a displayed list ··· Such use of colon is grammatically suspect and unnecessary.

  McCaskill M K. 1990. *Grammar, Punctuation, and Capitalization*, pp. 45–46. Hampton, Virginia: NASA Langley Research Center. 108 pp. [NASA SP-7084, available in PDF]

Lists
- Three or fewer simple items can be listed within a sentence.
- Four or more items are best presented as a bullet list ···
- As few as two (complex) items can be presented in a list.
- A single item should never be presented in a list.
- Each item in a list must have the same general form and use the same syntax.

  Pettersson R. 2002. *Information Design: an introduction*, p. 100. Amsterdam: John Benjamins. 296 pp.

✗ A typical reference citation should (a) identify the source precisely; (b) describe it sufficiently; and (c) guide the readers adequately if they wish to obtain the document.

✓ A typical reference citation should (a) identify the source precisely; (b) describe it sufficiently; and (c) guide the readers adequately if they wish to obtain the document.

Avoid ending a line with an item marker.

Lists embedded within text

Run-on lists are simple structures, formatted and punctuated the same way as continuous text, and the choice of item markers is limited to numbers or letters—bullets are never used in run-on lists. The recommended style is to use small letters within parentheses, as in 'A reference should (a) identify the source accurately; (b) describe it adequately; and (c) provide enough information about the source to obtain it easily.'

However, use numbers instead of small letters if the items in the list represent sequential steps in a process, as in 'To begin the process of installing a new font, (1) click on the Start button at the bottom left of the desktop screen; (2) choose Settings, followed by Control Panel; and (3) double-click on the Fonts folder.'

Here are a few points of style relevant to run-on lists.

- Do not use any punctuation to separate the verb that introduces a list from the list itself. In particular, do not insert a colon after such words as 'are' and 'including', which often introduce lists.
- Keep the list short; as a rule of thumb, a list of three or fewer items (Pettersson 2002) and running to no more than 40 words is appropriate—longer than that, and it is best to think of alternatives.
- Watch out for an item marker out on a limb, that is a marker falling at the end of a line and thus separated from the item itself, which is carried over to the next line. One way to prevent this is to use a 'non-breaking space' (Alt + 0160 in Windows) between the closing parenthesis of the marker and the first letter of the item.
- Punctuate the list so that each item is followed by a similar stop. Commas are usual but use semicolons if one or more items in the list already contain commas.

Apart from length, choice between the two types of lists, run-on or displayed, is often governed by contents. For example, a list that describes a step-by-step procedure is best set displayed. Also, if each item in the list is covered in detail

Chapter **3** Make a list

✗ Example

The objectives of the programme are
- prevention of land degradation
- building a large database
- to manage land resources

✓

The objectives of the programme are
- to prevent land degradation
- to build a large database
- to manage land resources

Make all items in a list structurally similar.

Example

Bullets for items without any particular order	Numbers for steps in a sequence	Letters for mutually exclusive choices
▸ _____	1 _____	a _____
▸ _____	2 _____	b _____
▸ _____	3 _____	c _____

Choose the item marker logically.

later, a displayed list serves as a useful miniature table of contents.

Keeping listed items parallel

If bullet points are to be effective, they must all share a common structure. It is not enough merely to format all the items the same way; they must all sound alike too—and keeping them 'parallel' in language and grammar is the only way to ensure that. Keep all items in a list similar in structure: make them all into questions, instructions/requests, phrases with no verb, or whatever.

It is a common error to use verbs with some items and nouns, particularly abstract nouns, with the others when writing a series of items.

Bullet lists for presentations must be concise. Because they are meant more as aide-memoires than as formal text, telegraphese is acceptable.

Choice of item markers

Item-markers are such devices as bullet points, dashes, and numbers, each of which signals a new item in a list. Let the contents of the list suggest which marker to use:

a   bullets when the order of the listed items has no particular significance (Walker and Taylor 1998, Kirkman 1999);
b   numbers when the items follow a definite order (steps of a process, for example); and
c   letters when the items represent mutually exclusive choices.

Never use dashes as markers: they are not conspicuous enough. Also, dashes serve a distinct function as marks of punctuation and are best reserved for that purpose. Do not use roman numerals either: they are difficult to align vertically.

Formatting of the item markers

Square bullets print more crisply than round bullets, especially on dot-matrix printers or low-resolution laser printers. Use medium-sized square bullets (■) or right-pointing triangles (▶)

✗	✓
7 ————	7 ————
8 ————	8 ————
9 ————	9 ————
10 ————	10 ————
11 ————	11 ————

Example

Align the numbers to the right to maintain a constant space between the numbers and the text.

> The distance between the dot point [bullet] and the first word of the entry (the indent) should be close enough to link the two, and to avoid the reader's eye having to travel too far to reach the first word of the text. But it should not be so close that the dot 'crowds' the text. A useful guide for the amount of horizontal space to leave between the dot and the text is at least a character space, but not more than an em space (the width of the lower-case letter 'm').
> Wiseman R. 1996. Bullet point lists.
> *Communication News* 9(2): 8–9

Quote

Example

(clear space underneath) (text underneath)

'Hanging' indents   'First-line' indents

as the first choice, keeping medium-size 'hollow' bullets (▫) for nested lists (lists within lists).

If you opt for letters or numbers as item markers, let them stand by themselves; do not enclose them within parentheses and do not type a full stop after them. In displayed lists, item markers stand out clearly because of the space that surrounds them; parentheses or full stops only add clutter. In a numbered list that runs to more than nine items, the numbers must be *right*-aligned.

Bullets or other item markers are made more conspicuous by surrounding them with empty space, namely (a) the horizontal space to the *right* of the marker and (b) the vertical space *below* the marker. In Microsoft Word, WordPerfect, and most other such software packages, the default gap between the bullet and the beginning of the item is half an inch, which is excessive. As Schriver (1997) puts it in *Dynamics in Document Design*, '··· avoid wide margins between the bullet and the text as the bullets may appear to form their own column.' If using such page layout programs as PageMaker or QuarkXPress, adjust the gap to an en space.

As to the space below, leave it clear of any text, a practice technically known as 'hanging indentation'. In other words, when the text of any item runs to two lines or more, the second and subsequent lines do not begin directly underneath a bullet but a little away from it, as seen in any list in this handbook.

Formatting a nested list

As far as possible, avoid using a list within a list. If you do, change three variables, namely (a) the item-marker, (b) the gap between the marker and the text of the item, and (c) the clear space below the item marker. Change them as follows.
▹ As an item marker, use a hollow bullet (▫) instead of a filled one (■).
▹ Make the gap between the bullet and the beginning of the text wider by using an em space. If that character is not available, insert an em dash (Alt + 0151) and change its colour

Example

narrower gap ↓

wider gap

text underneath

Mark a sub-list with 'hollow' bullets, a wider gap between the bullet and the text, and only first-line indents.

Quote

Avoid overpunctuating lists.
A list is an inherently spatial and numerical arrangement. Speakers reciting lists often enumerate on their fingers, and lists set in type often call for equivalent typographic gestures. This means that the list should be clarified as much as possible through spatial positioning and pointing, usually done with bullets, dashes or numerals.

Bringhurst R. 1996. *The Elements of Typographic Style*, 2nd edn, p. 71. Vancouver, Canada: Hartley & Marks. 350 pp.

to white so as to get a gap of the required width. Do not change the tab settings.
- Run the second and subsequent lines after the bulleted line directly underneath the bullet. In other words, do not use a hanging indent.

Punctuation in lists

Punctuate the list as you would punctuate normal running text. Begin each new item with a capital letter only if it begins a new sentence. Pay particular attention to sense: it is all too common to forget how the list was introduced; the text of the list then does not quite match the introductory phrase. Do not introduce any punctuation mark between the main verb and the rest of the sentence that follows it. If you start each item with a capital letter and end it with a full stop, you will be right most of the time. This is especially so when each item in the list runs to many words or contains more than one sentence.

If the items are short phrases (up to six words, as a rule of thumb), do not start them with a capital letter and do not put a full stop – or any mark at all, for that matter – at the end of each item. A comma or a semicolon can be used instead (whichever is appropriate) but it is unnecessary. Also, if you do use either of them, you need to end the last-but-one item with an 'and' (to keep up the pretence that the entire list is just one sentence). However, use a full stop at the end of the last item to mark the end of the entire list.

If the items in a list are all phrases or sentence fragments that are not a part of the introductory sentence, the last item cannot logically take a full stop—and it is pointless to add one.

Space between a list and surrounding text

The phrase or sentence that introduces a list, sometimes referred to as a 'stem sentence', and the list itself, are parts of a single paragraph, and the list usually ends that paragraph; the list is, therefore, closer in sense to the introductory phrase than to the matter that comes *after* the list. The conventional one-

> In terms of spacing, lists of points need to be visually linked with the paragraph to which they belong, yet to be separated clearly from the rest of the text in that paragraph. This can most easily be done by *not* leaving a line space between the rest of the paragraph and the list, and by indenting the text of the points.
>
> Simmonds D and Reynolds L. 1994. *Data Presentation and Visual Literacy in Medicine and Science*, p. 64. Oxford, UK: Butterworth-Heinemann. 192 pp.

> The results of this research confirm the critical role of the layout of lists in reading and understanding them. In Experiment 1, participants read one of four styles of a list and recalled. It was found that a separately arranged [displayed] list was recalled better than a continuously arranged list, and that the former was read more efficiently than the latter. The efficiency in reading was deemed to have affected the recall. Experiment 2 further examined reading processes for both text layouts. It was found that the separated list was reread more selectively and was thus understood faster than the continuous [run-on] one. The layout of a list clearly affected readers' access to information in text.
>
> Seki Y. 2000. Using lists to improve text access: the role of layout in reading. *Visible Language* **34**: 280–295

line gap between the introductory phrase and the list is therefore uncalled for. A half-line gap works well but creates another, albeit minor, problem: it pushes the text setting 'out of phase'; in other words, because of the half-line gap, lines of text printed on one side of a page may not back up with those printed on the reverse of that page. If you hold a printed page against bright light, you can check whether lines on both sides of a sheet are printed back to back. And because the list does not start a fresh paragraph, it should not start with a normal paragraph indent.

The length of a list

Lists owe a great deal of their impact to how they look on a page of text. Item markers are not simply decorative; they are crucial to the cohesive appearance of a list and identify it *at a glance* as a list. This visual impact is bound to be reduced, if not lost, if a list is so long that it sprawls over several pages. In general, therefore, a list should fit within a page (or two pages provided they face each other, forming a page-spread). Lists longer than that have either too many items, lengthy individual items, or both. If it is the first, see whether the contents can be presented as a table or as text set in multiple columns. If items are too long, consider presenting the contents as a series of paragraphs, each with a heading, instead of making an unwieldy list.

Typographic refinements

A bullet is normally so placed as to appear centred relative to the letter that follows it, which is usually a capital letter; if the following letter is not a capital letter, and especially at larger point sizes, a bullet will be out of alignment because it will appear to be a little higher than the letter that follows it. The result is particularly conspicuous with such short letters as a, c, and e or with letters that have descenders: g, j, p, q, and y. If so, lower the bullets slightly. The precise extent to which they need to be lowered would depend on the font; for 11-point Georgia, lower the bullets by 1.5 points.

> Address www.itcfonts.com/ulc/
> article.asp?nCo=AFMT&sec=ulc&issue=28.2.1&art=bullets
>
> Bullets should be centred on either the cap height or x-height, depending on the nature of your copy. If all of your items begin with a cap, center the bullet on the cap, or a bit lower ... If your items all begin with lower-case characters, centre the bullets on the x-height.
>
> Strizver I. 2001. Bullets [in the series 'For your typographic information] *U&lc Online*, 28 Feb. 2001

> Presentations do not need to be sophisticated. The favourite tool of the consulting profession, whether presenting proposals or delivering results, is a simple, old, tried and trusted favourite:
>
> the bullet point
>
> Where would consultants be without bullets, those eyes of flame that jump off the page and burn themselves into the consciousness of the client? At their best, they convey information with a crispness and concision which is hard to match. At their worst, they line up by their hundreds across hundreds of turgid slides, concussing the reader into the kind of persistent vegetative state that would have a doctor reaching for the off switch on the ventilator. Between those two extremes lie a multitude of wingdings.
>
> Ashford M. 1998. *Con Tricks: the shadowy world of management consultancy and how to make it work for you*, p. 139. London: Simon & Schuster. 298 pp.

> Address www.hcrc.ed.ac.uk/AnnualReport98/Text/
>
> ## Human Communication Research Centre
>
> Welcome to the home page of the Human Communication Research Centre (HCRC), an interdisciplinary research centre at the Universities of Edinburgh and Glasgow.
>
> ··· excessive bulleting of text seems to interfere with normal reading patterns and can lead to increased difficulty in finding information. On the other hand, the careful use of stem sentence bulleting does appear to produce advantages in document search with familiar documents. [Stem sentence bulleting refers to the use of text (a sentence or a phrase) to introduce the bullet list to follow.]
>
> Garrod S. 1998. Bullets for Auntie. *Annual Report 1998*. Glasgow, UK: Human Communication Research Centre.

The second refinement involves colour. A bullet is a dense mass of colour whereas letters not only consist of thinner strokes but also carry built-in empty spaces (the 'eye' of lower-case 'e', for instance). This makes bullets too prominent; if possible, make them grey instead of black (50% black, for instance).

References

Human Communication Research Centre. 1999
Bullets for auntie. 5 pp.
<www.hcrc.ed.ac.uk/AnnualReport98/Text/bull.html>

Kirkman J. 1999
Full Marks: advice on punctuation for scientific and technical writing, 3rd edn
Ramsbury, Wiltshire, UK: Ramsbury Books. 115 pp.

Pettersson R. 2002
Information Design: an introduction
Amsterdam: John Benjamins. 296 pp.

Schriver K A. 1997
Dynamics in Document Design: creating text for readers
New York: John Wiley. 560 pp.

Walker J R and Taylor T. 1998
The Columbia Guide to Online Style
New York: Columbia University Press. 218 pp.

Chapter **3** Make a list

Chapter 4 at a glance

Types of abbreviated forms
- Acronyms
- Contractions
- Symbols

When to use abbreviations
Explaining abbreviations
Abbreviations and capitals
Abbreviations, their plural forms, and the apostrophe
Abbreviations from languages other than English
Abbreviations: typographic refinements
Reference

4 ▶ Alphabet soup
abbreviations, acronyms, contractions, symbols

Dichlorodiphenyltrichloroethane is quite a mouthful—many would not even understand what you were talking about unless you said DDT; these days, when laser printers are common, not many will recall that laser is a device that uses light amplification by stimulated emission of radiation. Only specialists – and trivia buffs – would know that MIG (as in the aircraft) stands for Mikoyan i Gurevich (the 'i' is Russian for 'and'). Other such entities that are known more widely by the abbreviated form include AIDS and DNA and, if you go back further, even radar, which represents perhaps the last stage in the progression when the short version becomes a word in its own right. Thus, using shorter versions not only saves space but, at times, makes for clearer communication.

Technical writing is full of such shortened versions, whether they are acronyms, contractions, symbols, or any other variety. They are also the source of many fleeting moments of doubt that dog a writer, as evident from the following representative list of examples.

▶ Of the many documents published by UNESCO, some use that form and some use Unesco: which is correct?
▶ Which comes first, the shorter version or the spelt-out version? And which ones goes inside a pair of brackets?
▶ Is an apostrophe necessary to indicate plural forms of abbreviations? For instance, is it DVD's or DVDs?
▶ Since the shorter version is in capital letters, shouldn't capital letters be used when explaining the abbreviation? For instance, is RETs spelt out as 'renewable energy technologies' or 'Renewable Energy Technologies'?
▶ How are abbreviations explained when they are made up of letters that stand for words in a language other than English? GTZ, for example, is Gesellschaft für Technische Zusammenarbeit, which is German for the society for technical cooperation.

| Address | www.acronymfinder.com/ |

Resource

What's an acronym?
Here's an example of an acronym:
North Atlantic Treaty Organization = NATO.
An acronym is a pronounceable word formed from each of the first letters of a descriptive phrase. An acronym is actually a type of abbreviation. Our database contains abbreviations, acronyms, and initialisms and we make no distinction between them in our database or on our site. We are more interested in defining 'acronyms' for you than we are in trying to properly distinguish between abbreviations, acronyms, and initialisms.

| Address | www.acronymsearch.com/ |

Resource

Welcome to Acronym Search
Your source for acronyms and abbreviations

Enter the acronym to search for:
[Search]
Examples: NATO or ROFL or ASAP

Our database is updated every couple of days. There are over 40,000 acronyms and abbreviations in many categories. Including chat, computer, military, finance, accounting, airports, sports, classified, and more.

FAQ Topics:
What is an Acronym? | Acronym Grammar | Acronym Capitalization

Climate VISION stands for climate, voluntary innovative sector initiatives: opportunities now. Not since 2001's USA PATRIOT Act (uniting and strengthening America by providing appropriate tools required to intercept and obstruct terrorism) has an acronym been so contrived.
  New Scientist **177** (2384): p. 92 (*Feedback* column in the issue dated 1 March 2003)

Quote

These and related queries are discussed in this chapter, which explains some of the standard conventions in science publishing and specifies the style on related issues.

Types of abbreviated forms

So far, the phrase 'shorter version' has been used as a catch-all phrase to refer collectively to abbreviations, acronyms, contractions, symbols, and the like. But it is necessary to know how each is defined because style recommendations are often based on those distinctions: acronyms and contractions do not take a full stop; symbols admit no plurals (kg does duty both as a kilogram and kilograms—the form 'kgs' is definitely incorrect); acronyms are nearly always set in capital letters; and so on. 'Abbreviation' is often used as a residual term to include all shorter versions that are not acronyms, contractions, or symbols; this chapter uses the word in the same broad sense.

Acronyms

Acronyms are abbreviations that make a pronounceable word: OPEC or UNIDO, for instance. Abbreviated forms that are pronounced letter-by-letter (as in IQ, BBC, and OECD) do not qualify as acronyms (the term 'initialism' is sometimes used for this category). The distinction matters because pronunciation governs the choice of the indefinite article: referring to a member of parliament, we speak of 'an MP' because the two letters are pronounced separately and the first one begins with a vowel sound; referring to a compact disk, on the other hand, we say 'a CD' because the first letter does not begin with a vowel sound, just as we refer to 'a NATO exercise' or 'a Unicef project' because both forms are pronounceable words that do not begin with a vowel sound.

As an acronym comes into widespread use, it is more likely to be absorbed into the language and more so because it is pronounceable. In fact, the trend is to so choose words for the full version that they yield a handy acronym. As to UNESCO, the explanation is that the organization changed its preference from Unesco to UNESCO.

| Address | http://eur-op.eu.int/code/en/en-4100800en.htm | Quote |

Note the difference between a true abbreviation, in which the end of the word is lopped off (vol., co., inc.) and a contraction or suspension, in which the interior of the word is removed (Mr, Dr, contd, Ltd). The contraction is always printed without the final full point, whereas the abbreviation retains it.

| Address | <www.hum.ku.dk/ami/mjd/thoughts.html> | Quote |

Then there are 'backronyms', words which are interpreted as acronyms although they were not originally so intended. Twain, the name of the scanner interface standard, for example, was apparently taken from Kipling's 'and never the twain shall meet', but the large number of acronyms in the computer industry led people to assume that Twain, especially when the TWAIN standards organization decided to start spelling it in all uppercase, must also be one. But what could it stand for? One suggestion was 'Technology Without An Interesting Name'. ...

Driscoll M J. 2002. Stray thoughts on abbreviations in some modern European languages, in *Grace-notes played for Michael Chesnutt on the occasion of his 60th birthday, 18 September 2002.*

Contractions

Contractions form another special category of abbreviations in which the shortened version is 'carved out' of the full version. As a result, the first letter of the shortened version is the same as the first letter of the full version and the last letters of both versions are also the same, as in Mr and Mister or Dr and Doctor or Dept and Department, in all of which the usual dot that marks an abbreviation is dispensed with. This is why, in the style recommended in this handbook, Dr and Mr do not take a dot but Pvt. does. The distinction between an abbreviation and a contraction is far more common in Britain but seldom followed in the United States.

The exception to the rule that contractions do not end with a full point is a contraction that happens to be a separate word by itself, as in 'no' and 'no.' (for the Italian 'numero'). As Carey (1958) puts it in *Mind the Stop: a brief guide to punctuation*, 'a coy commander is different from a coy. [for company] commander.

Symbols

Many symbols are sufficiently distinctive and pose no problem. Their distinct appearance prevents us from using them as ordinary words: they cannot form plurals or combine with other words. Take the symbol for the dollar: the symbol $ does duty both as dollar and dollars; you do not write $s to mean dollars. Similarly, it is either µg or microgram/s but never µgram. However, when ordinary letters of the alphabet double as symbols, they pose problems because rules for the use of symbols are precise and strict; those for abbreviations are not. This accounts for the most common violation of scientific style, namely attaching 's' to a symbol to form a plural (as in kgs for kilograms or kms for kilometres). It is wrong because km is not an abbreviation for kilometre, though it certainly looks like one, but a combination of symbols, namely k (for a thousand times) and m (for metre), which follow well-defined rules when they combine. This matter is dealt with in greater detail in the next chapter, which covers the standard notation for units of measurement.

| Address | http://www.chsrf.ca/docs/resource/cn-selfedit_e.pdf |

> Even if someone knows, or works out, or you told them at the beginning of the paper what an acronym means, they're hard to read. Acronyms are like boulders on a path — they may not actually trip you, but climbing over them still slows you down. The rule is concepts should never be expressed as acronyms; don't say "MI" for mentally ill or LOS for length of stay. Organizations may sometimes be referred to by their acronym, but the first reference must always be spelled out ···
>
> Canadian Health Services Research Foundation. 2001. Self-Editing: putting your readers first. [*Communication Notes* series]

> First, never use an abbreviation in the title of an article. Very few journals allow abbreviations in titles, and their use is strongly discouraged by the indexing and abstracting services. ···
>
> Abbreviations should almost never be used in the Abstract. Only if you use the same name, a long one, quite a number of times should you consider an abbreviation. If you use an abbreviation, you must define it at the first use in the abstract. ···
>
> Do not abbreviate a term that is used only a few times in the paper. If the term is used with modest frequency — let us say between three and six times — and a standard abbreviation for that term exists, introduce and use the abbreviation.
>
> Day R A. 1995. *How to Write and Publish a Scientific Paper*, 4th edn, pp. 180–181. Cambridge, U K: Cambridge University Press. 223 pp.

> When introducing an acronym on first mention would interrupt a compound or force an otherwise awkward parenthetical expression, either the sentence should be rewritten or the introduction of the acronym should be delayed until the second mention of the term.
>
> Einsohn A. 2000. *The Copyeditor's Handbook: a guide for book publishing and corporate communications*, p. 227. Berkeley, California, U S A: University of California Press. 560 pp.

When to use abbreviations

Do not use abbreviations as a matter of course. You do not have to offer the abbreviated version at all if it does not occur in the text ever again or if you are not going to use it often, no matter how common it is in your field. Though abbreviations save space, that saving must not be at the cost of readability. Abbreviations, together with jargon, are often the most common hurdles that general readers face while reading anything technical. Therefore, use abbreviations sparingly. It is better to write 'billion cubic metres' instead of BCM or 'tonnes per day' instead of tpd and so on, unless you are writing exclusively for specialists.

Secondly, the same abbreviation may mean different things to different people. I remember even now the puzzled expression of an American visitor to Delhi, who wanted to know what services were on offer at the STD booths he saw everywhere because to him STD meant sexually transmitted diseases and not subscriber trunk dialling!

Rigid insistence on explaining an abbreviation only once and using it throughout the text thereafter makes for consistency but often hinders comprehension: readers may not remember the explanation they saw dozens of pages earlier. In reference books, it is common to print a list of abbreviations and their spelt-out versions on a separate page that users can find readily (on the inside of the front cover, for instance). You may choose to explain abbreviations afresh in each chapter, especially in a collection of specialized papers that few would read from cover to cover. Use your judgement in such situations.

Judgement is also needed when citing references to documents attributed to organizations instead of named individuals, as in documents published by the Central Pollution Control Board, Forest Survey of India, Environmental Protection Agency, and so on. The choice is between using such forms as CPCB 1998 and Central Pollution Control Board 1998 because for those in the field, the initialism is familiar enough whereas for others, it is just a string of characters: all it means to them is

> It makes little difference whether you cite the abbreviation first and then put the full name in parentheses, or whether you do it the other way around; it's largely a matter of style. ··· The use of an abbreviation indicates that you plan to reuse the term and want your readers to recognize it.
> Judd K. 1990. *Copyediting: a practical guide*, 2nd edn, p. 161. Los Altos, California, U S A: Crisp Publications. 317 pp.

> Use parentheses to enclose explanations of acronyms formed from groups of words, if you are going to use *the acronym* throughout your text: ··· decision was taken to use GRP (glass-reinforced plastic). Two suppliers of GRP have been ···
> Use parentheses to enclose the acronym formed from groups of words, if you are going to use *the words* throughout your text.
> Kirkman J. 1999. *Full Marks: advice on punctuation for scientific and technical writing*, 3rd edn. Ramsbury, Wiltshire, U K: Ramsbury Books. 115 pp.

The energy produced at each stage of the oxidative cycle is in a form familiarly spoken of by the biochemists as ATP (adenosine triphosphate), a molecule containing three phosphate groups.

Use the abbreviated version first and follow it up with the full version in brackets.

| Address | www.kanten.com/styleguide/ |

> An unfamiliar acronym or abbreviation that will appear numerous times in a document should be clarified by enclosing its unabbreviated form within parentheses after its first use:
> The aims of the WRC (Women's Relief Corps) were to aid and memorialize the GAR (Grand Army of the Republic).
> Placing the unabbreviated form first (and the acronym in parentheses) is not incorrect, but it may inhibit reader comprehension since the acronym will not be enclosed in parentheses in the remainder of the document.

that it is a document by 'a corporate author', as cataloguers would put it. You must use only one form throughout because that form would decide where the full reference will be when references are arranged alphabetically and yet it is important to give readers some idea of the source that is being cited. Judgement comes in because your choice will be influenced by your guess: Will most of your readers be familiar with the short version?

One solution is to use the abbreviation throughout but to explain it the first time *in a footnote*.

Explaining abbreviations

Use the abbreviation and follow it up with an explanation in parentheses: 'dpi (dots per inch) is a measure of how finely a laser printer will print an image or text.' Note the sequence: the abbreviation first and the explanation later. Giving the spelt-out version after the short version is uncommon but this handbook recommends the style because its is logical and reader-friendly.

Parentheses signal that the matter they enclose is incidental or secondary — readers may skip it if they wish. Putting the explanation in parentheses is consistent with this usage.

Some maintain that when the definition comes first, the association with its abbreviation sinks in and is carried forward. However, consider how we learn new words or unfamiliar terms: we see them used and construct what they mean from the context or look them up in a dictionary or a glossary. Those who know the term will simply skip the explanation whereas for those who do not, help is ready to hand. Secondly, an unfamiliar sequence of letters primes the brain to look for an explanation and thus facilitates learning when the explanation is presented (the same principle of active learning that makes it more likely that you will remember the way to a new location if you know that the next time around you will be on your own, as compared with the passive learning that takes place when such motivation is missing).

Chapter 4 Alphabet soup

> The purpose of EIA (environmental impact assessment) is to evaluate the beneficial and adverse effects of the proposed activity on the environment.
> Successive generation of people in bunches, never seeming well organized, have been building the MBL (Marine Biological Laboratory) since it was chartered in 1888.

Set acronyms in capital letters but use lower-case letters to explain the acronym—*unless* the acronym is used as a proper noun, a name of an organization, for instance. Do not highlight the initial letters by making them bold or setting them in italics—trust your readers.

For some, but not all, abbreviations, case is important; that is, if they are capitalized, they must never be made lower-case; if they are lower-case, they must never be capitalized. This guideline applies to abbreviations that would lose their meanings or change if their forms are changed, such as units of measure (e.g., mg cannot be changed to Mg, min cannot be changed to Min), mathematical symbols ⋯ and chemical symbols (e.g. *o* for ortho cannot be changed to *O*).

Dodd J S (ed.). 1997. *The ACS Style Guide: a manual for authors and editors*, 2nd edn, pp. 101–102. Washington, DC: American Chemical Society. 460 pp.

Though once commonly used in the plural of abbreviations and numerals (*QC's, the 1960's*), the apostrophe is now best omitted in such circumstances: *MAs, MPs, the 1980s, the three Rs*, ⋯

Burchfield R W (ed.). 1996. *The New Fowler's Modern English Usage*, p. 61. Oxford, UK: Oxford University Press. 864 pp.

✗ Audio CD's offer better-quality sound than audio tapes.
✓ Audio CDs offer better-quality sound than audio tapes.

Omit the apostrophe in plurals of abbreviations.

Abbreviations and capitals

Use capitals only when grammar requires it (as with proper nouns). Use capitals for the abbreviation but not for its explanation unless it represents a proper noun (most commonly, the formal name of an organization). Thus, write MTOE (million tonnes of oil equivalent) but MOEF (the Ministry of Environment and Forests). The concept of joint forest management is precisely that—a concept. And that does not qualify for capitalizing it when offered as an explanation: so it is JFM (joint forest management). The argument that it is very widely known is irrelevant: ELISA (enzyme-linked immunosorbent assay) is a widely used technique in immunology but that does not make it Enzyme Linked Immuno Sorbent Assay.

By convention, some abbreviations are always set in small letters (rpm and dpi, for example). Again, what is familiar to you may not be so to your readers (rpm is also 'resale price maintenance'). When in doubt, consult a good, current, general-purpose dictionary (the *New Oxford Dictionary of English*, published in 1998, is particularly recommended) or follow the usage of a standard journal in your field if you are writing for possible publication in a journal.

Words such as iMac and eBay may look like abbreviations but they are not; they are proper nouns and retain their mixed capitalization (variously known as intercaps, camel case, and Pascal case). Short versions are also created by bumping words together to form a single word with internal capitals (as in PowerPoint, WordPerfect, and PricewaterhouseCoopers). Again, these forms are not strictly abbreviations.

Abbreviations, their plural forms, and the apostrophe

Do not use the apostrophe to indicate plurals. Often the same abbreviation covers both singular and plural forms, as in DBMS (for database management system/s); the context makes it clear which form is being used.

> You must also consider readers from outside your own interests, and those whose first language is not yours, who may have familiar abbreviations based on words in their language: in French NATO is OTAN, and AIDS is SIDA.
>
> Goodman N W and Edwards M B. 1997. *Medical Writing: a prescription for clarity*, 2nd edn, p. 167. Cambridge, UK: Cambridge University Press. 223 pp.

> Text set in all capital letters (whether full-sized capitals or small capitals) needs a more generous horizontal spacing allowance than text set in capitals and lower-case to ensure that individual character shapes are clear. Increased character spacing usually improves the appearance of capitals and small capitals. But it should be used with caution where the capitals are embedded in text (for example, in formulae or abbreviations) in case it disrupts the overall texture of the text.
>
> Black A. 1990. *Typefaces for Desktop Publishing: a user guide*, p. 16. London: Architecture Design and Technology Press. 106 pp.

Abbreviations from languages other than English

Such common abbreviations as e. g. (*exempli gratia*, Latin for 'for the sake of example'), etc. (*et cetera*, Latin for 'and the rest'), et al. (*et alii* or *et aliae*, Latin for 'and others', masculine and feminine respectively), and RSVP (*répondez s'il vous plaît*, French for 'please reply') have virtually attained the status of symbols in the sense that they are always used in a fixed form and never have to be explained in any document, technical or otherwise. However, other abbreviations, especially those that stand for names of organizations, are not so entrenched as to require no explanation.

Whether and how you should spell out abbreviations of words in languages other than English – names of organizations is a common instance – depends on how much explaining you consider necessary or useful to the intended readers. The recommended form is to supply the full version in the original language, followed by its English translation, as in GTZ (Gesellschaft für Technische Zusammenarbeit, German for the society for technical cooperation) or CERN (Conseil Européen pour la Recherche Nucléaire, French for the European organization for nuclear research). Note that in the translation, it is not necessary to capitalize each word. In publicity literature such as conference flyers, brochures, and announcements, where the abbreviation is usually accompanied by the organization's logo and address, translation is superfluous: in acknowledgements and elsewhere within the body of a report or a book, translation is essential.

Abbreviations: typographic refinements

You may have noticed that the capital letters in all the abbreviations used as examples in this chapter are slightly spaced out, as in CERN instead of CERN. The style is traditional in all good typography; it compensates for the loss in readability of any matter set entirely in capitals: spacing the letters out makes the shape of each more distinct. Secondly, a profusion of such clusters of capital letters makes the page look

Chapter 4 Alphabet soup

Reliable data on the existing quality of ambient air are required for any effective strategy to control air pollution. CPCB (Central Pollution Control Board) launched the NAAQM (national ambient air quality monitoring) programme in 1984 with 28 stations in seven cities.

Example

Reliable data on the existing quality of ambient air are required for any effective strategy to control air pollution. CPCB (Central Pollution Control Board) launched the NAAQM (national ambient air quality monitoring) programme in 1984 with 28 stations in seven cities.

Formatted small capitals (top) and true small capitals (bottom)

··· small caps are a particularly useful alternative when a text has many acronyms. Small caps are not just smaller sizes of a full cap; they are specially designed letters, their weight matching that of the rest of the font. Reducing the size of capital letters to simulate small caps simply will not do.
Hendel R. 1998. *On Book Design*, p. 43–44. New Haven, Connecticut, USA: Yale University Press. 210 pp.

Quote

Real small caps are different from computer-compressed capitals, which look like they were washed in water that was too hot. ··· If someone loses twenty pounds, then his or her figure will have different proportions. It's not any different when small caps are made out of caps. ··· Real small caps have been designed by type designers so that a smooth and harmonious type picture is portrayed. This involves line weight, spacing, and several other characteristics. Today, many digitized typefaces include real small caps. They can be found as Small Cap Fonts, in Expert Sets, and they are easy as pie to access.
Rögner S, Pool A, and Packhäuser U. 1995. *Branding with Type*, pp. 74–75. Mountain View, California, USA: Adobe Press. 120 pp. [Translated from German by S Tripier, edited by E M Ginger]

Quote

spotty; separating them with a little extra space reduces this effect. Such letterspacing, as the practice is known, has another functional advantage as well: it prevents readers from mistaking the shortened versions for ordinary words, spelt identically, set in capitals (mistaking WHO, the World Health Organization, for the pronoun who, for example).

A further refinement is to use 'small capitals' for the purpose but only if they are available as a separate character set. In true small capitals, the shape of each letter is the same as that of the corresponding regular capital. However, if you observe how thickly they are drawn, you will notice that true small capitals are drawn as thick as the small letters, which are slightly thicker than capital letters. If you type out an acronym in only capital letters and choose the option 'small caps' in the Font menu, all that the program does is to replace the letters with those set in a slightly smaller font size: it does not make them any thicker. As a result, the group of letters actually looks a little lighter. Contrast this with the letters set in true small caps, which blend harmoniously with the rest of the text.

Unfortunately, fonts with true small capitals are neither freely available nor do they come bundled with or pre-installed with operating systems such as Windows 2000. Therefore, it is better to avoid using small capitals altogether and space out the capital letters instead.

Reference

Carey G V. 1958
Mind the Stop: *a brief guide to punctuation with a note on proof-correction*
Harmondsworth, UK: Penguin Books. 126 pp.

Chapter 5 at a glance

Numbers: general
Dates and time
Symbols and prefixes
Abbreviations
Repetition of symbols
Special characters
Currency symbols
Geographic coordinates
References

5 ▶ How long is a piece of string?

notation for units of measurement

What is the difference between symbols and abbreviations? A small 'g' is the symbol for gram, a unit of measurement, but 'gm' is an abbreviation—and a non-standard one at that. Such symbols as 'g' for the gram and 'm' for the metre, though they look like ordinary letters of the alphabet, behave like symbols such as *, $, and @ in that they have a fixed physical form and cannot form plurals: you can write asterisks but not '*s'; in the same way, it is incorrect to write gs or gms for grams. This chapter supplies some information on representing physical quantities, which you may find useful in dealing with such typical queries as those listed below.

▶ What is the symbol for hour, 'h' or 'hr'?
▶ How should thousands be separated, with a comma or with a space?
▶ Should the unit be repeated in spans or ranges (12–15 kg or 12 kg – 15 kg)?
▶ When is it appropriate to express sums of rupees in lakhs and crores?
▶ What is the recommended notation for geographic coordinates (latitude and longitude)?

The purpose of any notation is unambiguous communication—but who are the parties engaged in communication? They matter because they influence the choice of units and notation. A typographer communicating with other typographers can get away with saying 'use a margin 5 picas wide' but most others would find a width of 21 millimetres far easier to understand and visualize. Physical scientists talk of, say, 12 Tg (teragrams) of carbon but economists would say 12 million tonnes instead. Thus, choosing an appropriate unit is far from a straightforward matter.

> **Address** www.xencraft.com/resources/multi-currency.html#formats

> **Grouping separator**
> The integer portion of a number is often split into groups by a grouping separator. Western numbers generally separate numbers into thousands, or groups of 3 digits. However, other styles exist. Older Chinese and Japanese number systems grouped 4 digits (groups of ten thousand). Indian number format groups the lowest order 3 digits (thousands) and then every 2 digits after that.
>
> | Culture | Example | Grouping |
> |---|---|---|
> | British | 1,234,567,890.12 | Groups of 3 |
> | Old Japanese | 1,2345.67 | Groups of 4 |
> | Indian | 12,34,56,789.01 | One group of 3, then groups of 2 |
> | German | 12.345,67 | Group separator is full-stop |
> | French | 12 345,67 | Group separator is space |

> Correspondence courses ··· are already being conducted by 22 universities, with an enrolment of 1,15,000.
>   Let us leave aside for a moment how this would sound if the last figure was given orally. As written, it constitutes a puzzle for anyone outside the Indian subcontinent ··· Elsewhere, if commas are used in long figures, they separate units of three digits counting from the right. In such cultures, [the] figure looks like a misprint: is the first comma to be deleted or is there a digit missing between the two commas? The fact is, of course, there is no error: the method of punctuating the digits reflects precisely the Indian mode of referring to units larger than a thousand. The quantity that the rest of us refer to analytically as 'a hundred thousand' is for Indians lexicalised as a *lakh* a hundred of which in turn is lexicalised as a *crore*.
>   Quirk R. 1986. *Words at Work: lectures on textual structure*, p. 23. London: Longman. 137 pp.

Example

1 027 015 247

12 791 458

Present 5-digit or longer numbers in groups of threes; separate the groups with a non-breaking space.

Handling large numbers

Symbols and abbreviations also pose problems because there is no one standard. For instance, 'L' for litres is common only in the US and Canada. Germans often use a comma where others would use a decimal point (a book published by Springer-Verlag priced at DM 20,00 costs 20 Deutschmarks and not 2000). Even the so-called 'thousands separator' – a comma in the US and a space in Britain – can lead to confusion because, in India, it is commonly used to separate crores, lakhs, and thousands. For instance, the latest census gives the exact figure for the population of Delhi (about 12 million in April 2001) as 12,791,458, which is commonly rendered as 1,27,91,458 (and read out as 1 crore, 27 lakh, 91 thousand ···).

Some publishers prefer negative exponents for expressing rates: 12 kmph (kilometres per hour) is expressed as 12 km h^{-1} where others use km/h. Therefore, it is best to follow the style recommended by the publisher.

The following suggestions apply to project reports and articles for a general audience and include only those items that are used more frequently. Two useful references are *Quantities, Units and Symbols* (Royal Society 1975) and *Changing to the Metric System* (Anderton and Bigg 1972). The (US) National Institute of Standards and Technology guidelines are available at <http://physics.nist.gov/cuu/Units/index.html> and offer a great deal of background information.

Numbers: general

> Prefer millions and billions to lakhs and crores. If numbers are in lakhs, divide by ten to get millions; if in crores, multiply by ten instead. However, for documents meant specifically for readers within the Indian subcontinent (such as proposals submitted to government ministries), use lakhs and crores and group the digits accordingly, separating them with commas (as in Rs 2,34,000 for two lakh thirty-four thousand rupees); for an international audience, print the figure as Rs 234 000 (to mean two hundred and thirty-four thousand rupees).

Chapter 5 How long is a piece of string?

Address: www.joshmadison.com/software/convert/ *Resource*

Convert is an easy-to-use unit conversion program that will convert the most popular units of distance, temperature, volume, and many others, including the ability to create custom conversions.

About the order of date figures ··· We need to know how many dollars more immediately than how many cents, how many metres before how many millimetres, how many hundreds before how many tens. But with chronology, most of us in diurnal conversation and communication want to know the day first and foremost; then the month and if are referring to longer periods, the year. ··· It is simply a question of getting the information most of us need most of the time as immediately and simply as possible.
    Farmer P. 2002. *Australian Style* 10(2): 7. [In Letters to the Editor, in response to the article in the previous issue by Pat Naughtin, titled 'Is 07 04 2002 the 4th of July?' recommending the all-numeric yyyy mm dd format] *Quote*

✓	✗	✗	✗	✓	✗
15 August 1947	15 Aug., 1947	15th	15th	2 October	02 October
✗	✓	✗	✓	✗	✓
'03	2003	650 AD	AD 650	BC 900	900 BC

Example

Address: http://www.guardian.co.uk/styleguide *Quote*

BC goes after the date or century, e.g. 55 BC; AD goes before the figure (AD 64) but after the century: second century AD (or BC)
    Marsh D and Marshall N. 2002. *The Guardian Style Guide*, p. 13. London: Guardian. 133 pp.

SI units, date, and time

- Do not use such non-SI (Système International d'Unités) units as pounds, tons, inches and miles, acres, and barrels. If this is not possible, provide appropriate conversion factors (1 barrel of fuel oil = 0.149 tonne, and so on).
- Choose an appropriate multiplier or divider so as to keep the numerical value between 0.1 and 100 (2 km instead of 2000 m, and so on). Exceptions to this general recommendation include oceanic depths and heights at which aircraft fly (always given in metres), and the speed of light.
- Use a non-breaking space and not a comma as a 'thousands separator'. Use it for all numbers larger than four digits. However, when numbers are arranged in columns and both 4-digit numbers and larger numbers occur within a single column, use a thousands separator with the 4-digit numbers also, so that all the numbers align properly. See the section 'Special characters' (p. 71) to find out how to insert a non-breaking space.
- Repeat the per cent sign (%) as many times as required: 37%, 40%, and 57% not 37, 40, and 57%. Set the per cent sign close up (4% not 4 %).

Dates and time

- Use the day-month-year format for dates. Skip the comma after the month. Do not insert a leading zero in a single-digit date (9 June not 09 June). Avoid cardinal forms (9 June not 9th June nor 9th June).
- Give years in the 4-digit form; do not use an inverted comma for the first two digits (1998 not '98). If you want to use AD with years, place it *before* the year: AD 2001 not 2001 AD (but BC comes *after* the year: 400 BC).
- Use a decimal for the 12-hour clock. Use 12 noon or 12 m (not 12 p.m.) for midday and 12 midnight for 12 a.m. It is better to use the terms 'early morning' and 'late evening' and make it easier for readers than to use, for instance, 1.25 a.m. or 11.50 p.m. Put a colon between the hours and minutes (14:47 for 2.47 p.m., and so on) if you are using the 24-hour clock.

> Here are some conventional uses of the colon.
> In times, to separate hours from minutes, especially in American usage:
> 9:30   14:15
> Periods are more usual in British usage, but colons are always used for the 24-hour clock.
>> Greenbaum S. 1996. *The Oxford English Grammar*, p. 526. Oxford: Oxford University Press. 652 pp.

Example:

2.47 p.m.   14:47 hours

✗ ✓ ✓ ✓
12 p.m.   12 noon   12 m   12:00 hours

✗ ✓ ✓
12 a.m.   12 midnight   24:00 hours

Example:

2003/04 (1 April 2003 to 31 March 2004, the Indian fiscal year)
Use a slash to indicate a 12-month period comprising portions from two consecutive calendar years.

Example:

✗ ✓ ✓ ✓
65 kgs   65 kg   65 kilograms   65 kilos

✗ ✓ ✓
18 gms   18 g   18 grams

Do not use plural forms for symbols.

| Address | www.bipm.fr/enus/6_Publications/si/si-brochure.html |

> SI unit symbols (and also many non-SI unit symbols) are written as follows.
> - Roman (upright) type is used for the unit symbols. In general, unit symbols are written in lower case, but, if the name of the unit is derived from the proper name of a person, the first letter of the symbol is a capital.
> - When the name of a unit is spelled out, it is always written in lower case, except when the name is the first word of a sentence or is the name 'degree Celsius'.
> - Unit symbols are unaltered in the plural.
> - Unit symbols are not followed by a full stop (period), except as normal punctuation at the end of a sentence.
>> Bureau International des Poids et Mesures. 1998. *The International System of Units*, 7th edn, p. 109. Paris: BIPM. 152 pp.

- Use a slash to indicate a financial year: 1998/99 means, in India, the period from 1 April 1998 to 31 March 1999.

Symbols and prefixes

- Symbols have no plurals. The base units – g for gram, m for metre, and s for second – are represented by single letters; they have no plural form. By adding appropriate prefixes (multipliers), the value of any unit is multiplied in steps of one thousand: k (kilo) multiplies the value by a thousand (1 kg = 1000 g); M (mega), by a million (1 MW = 1000 kW); and G (giga), by a billion (1 GW = 1000 MW).
- Similarly, a prefix can divide the value in steps of one thousand: m (milli, or one-thousandth) divides it by 1000 (1 mm = 1/1000 metre), µ (micro – lower-case Greek 'mu' – or one-millionth) divides it by a million (1 µg or a microgram is one-millionth of a gram), and so on.
- Symbols for quantities that are named after people take capitals, as in W for watt (after James Watt) and N for newton (after Sir Isaac Newton) but do not retain the capitals when the word is spelt out in full (except degrees Celsius).
- All dividers take the lower case, and so do multipliers up to the kilo (hence kWh and not KWh). Multipliers from 'mega' onwards are set in capitals, as in MW (megawatts), GJ (gigajoules), and Tg (teragrams).

Abbreviations

- Spell out litres in full: 34 litres and not 34 l, to prevent it being misread for the numeral one. The alternative, which is standard and far more common in USA and Canada, is to use L as the symbol for the litre.
- If you are required to use 'million tonnes' very often within a document, explain the abbreviation when you use it for the first time and use 'mt' thereafter. The same holds good for million hectares (mha) and billion cubic metres (bcm)

Chapter **5** How long is a piece of string?

> **Address** www.pnl.gov/ag/usage/metrics.html
>
> When written as a symbol, the exponent (or superscript) 2 follows the unit symbol; when written as words, the term 'square' is placed in front of the unit to indicate area, and 'squared' is written after the unit for other operations. ··· When written as words, the term 'cubic' is placed in front of the unit to indicate volume, as in cubic centimeter; otherwise, the term 'cubed' is written after the unit. Do not mix exponent symbols with words. For example, meter² is incorrect; either write the term as square meter or use the symbol m².
>
> Sudikatus G. 1996. Metrics the right way. Authors Guide. Richland, Washington, USA: Pacific Northwest Laboratory.

Quote

41–60 kg   4 × 4 × 4 m

41 kg to 60 kg   4 m by 4 m by 4 m

Use the unit symbols only once in expressions that use other symbols (dash, multiplication sign); otherwise, repeat the unit symbols.

Example

✗   ✓

328 million sq.km   328 million square kilometres

5.2 bcm   5.2 billion cubic metres

3 280 000 kilometre²   3 280 000 km²

Avoid using symbols in expressions that use other abbreviations such as 'sq.' for square, 'b' for billion, and 'c' for cubic. Use exponents with symbols when space is limited.

Example

Abbreviations, special characters

though, in all such cases, million tonnes, million hectares, billion cubic metres, etc. are to be preferred.

- Avoid cu.m. for cubic metres: either spell it out in full or use m^3. Similarly, use square kilometres or km^2. The notation using superscripts is particularly handy in tables.
- The symbol for hour is simply h and not hr and that for year is simply y and not yr. However, you may want to spell out the word in full (hour, year, etc.) if you are writing for a broader readership.
- Such notations as MTOE (million tonnes of oil equivalent) and tpa (tonnes per annum) are standard in industry and economics and quite in order in technical reports though they are rarely used in the physical sciences.
- You could use the 'Insert → Symbol → Special Characters' route to insert such symbols as Greek letters. However, it is better to use the Alt + the 4-digit code (from the numerical keypad) route because this method ensures that the characters are reproduced within all Windows applications (PowerPoint, CorelDraw, or whatever) whereas characters inserted using the 'Insert → Symbol → Special Characters' route may be specific only to Microsoft Word.

Repetition of symbols

Use the unit symbol only once with the en dash (30–35 °C not 30 °C–35 °C) or with the multiplication symbol when giving the dimensions (a 4 × 4 cm piece of paper). With such words as 'to' and 'by', repeat the symbol as often as necessary: 30 °C to 35 °C, 4 cm by 4 cm.

Special characters

Non-breaking space Insert a non-breaking space between the number and the unit. In Windows, a non-breaking space is inserted by pressing Alt and typing 0160 (from the numerical keypad, with NumLock on). This will always keep the value and the unit together.

> When two or more countries use the same name for their currencies, the appropriate distinguishing adjective should be used at first mention, or throughout the text if confusion is possible: two million Irish pounds, six million pounds sterling. When the monetary unit is written in full, it should follow the number for the amount, as in the examples above, but when the abbreviation is used to represent the monetary unit, there should be no space between the symbol and amount ··· Where the abbreviation is a letter or letters or a combination of letter(s) and symbol, there should be one space between the abbreviation and the amount ···
>
> Office of Publications. 1998. *WHO Editorial Style Manual*, p. 44. Geneva: World Health Organization. 116 pp.

USD 123 or $123   GBP 123 or £123   EUR 123 or €123

Insert a space between currency *abbreviations* and the value; place currency *symbols* close to the value.

> Address: www.xe.com/iso4217.htm
>
> In most cases, the currency code is composed of the country's two-character Internet country code plus an extra character to denote the currency unit. For example, the code for Canadian dollars is simply Canada's two-character internet code ('CA') plus a one-character currency designator ('D').

En dash Use the longer dash (the en dash; Alt + 0150 in Windows) to indicate spans: 12–15 days for 12 to 15 days, 1980/81 – 1989/90 for the 10-year period, and so on.

Degree sign Use a proper degree symbol, not a superscript 'o' or zero. The sign and the capital C (for Celsius) go together (24 °C and not 24° C).

Multiplication sign Use the proper multiplication sign (×) and not the letter 'x'.

Currency symbols

Separate currency *abbreviations* from the value with a non-breaking space (Rs 100 not Rs100) but type currency *symbols* close to the value ($100 not $ 100). With large quantities of money, avoid both: 5 million rupees (not Rs 5 million) and 10 billion dollars (not $10 billion). The use of 3-letter codes for currencies (USD, GBP, INR, etc.) is becoming increasingly common, and has the merit of avoiding the use of special symbols.

Geographic coordinates

Set geographic coordinates thus: 28°37′ N, 77°13′ E. Note the use of the degree symbol and the use of prime for minutes. All are set close, without any space. The latitude (N or S) is always given first and the longitude (E or W) last, and the two are separated by a comma.

References

Anderton P and Bigg P H. 1972
Changing to the Metric System*: conversion factors, symbols and definitions*
London: Her Majesty's Stationery Office. 58 pp.

Royal Society. 1975
Quantities, Units and Symbols, 2nd edn
London: The Royal Society. 54 pp.

Chapter **5** How long is a piece of string?

Chapter 6 at a glance

Simple, open, or informal tables
Effective organization of data
Referring to a table in continuous text
Scheme for numbering tables
Titles of tables
General note/s to a table
Column heads
Body of the column
Row headings
Horizontal alignment within a row
Notation for missing values
Footnotes
Source/s
Table design and format
Positioning tables within text pages
Landscape tables
Tables split across more than one page
The 'Continued' line
Large tables that cannot fit within a normal page
References

6 ▶ Setting the table

presenting information in rows and columns

Visualize a table that gives information on, say, the average monthly maximum temperatures in four Indian cities: Ahmedabad, Bangalore, Delhi, and Hyderabad. Set in a standard format used for tables, the table would be roughly 7 cm wide and 10 cm tall, an area of 70 square centimetres. Now, consider the amount of information that the table holds. What is the maximum temperature in Delhi in, say, April? Or in Bangalore in December? Which is the coolest month in Hyderabad? Put this way, the table holds a great deal of information, which will easily fill a page if presented in words as running text.

This example highlights how tables compress information. If you keep this in mind, you will probably be more receptive to the rest of the discussion in this chapter, which attempts to describe – in excruciating detail – how tables may be constructed to make them user-friendly. You will also find answers to many relevant questions such as those listed here.

▶ Can the line that gives the title of a table be wider than the body of the table?
▶ Which is the best position for a table already referred to in the text?
▶ What notation is used to indicate that data for some of the cells in a table are not available?
▶ How are sources of data acknowledged?
▶ Do the titles of tables end with a full stop?

Because tables are so densely packed with information, their format needs to be particularly considerate. Extracting information from tables usually occurs in two stages. First, readers try to get the broad picture: What is the table all about? How is it organized? What do all these numbers mean? Next, users

··· good tables and diagrams are not born without pain. They require at least as much effort as the sentences of the text. An author may revise the text repeatedly, in order to improve the presentation, yet may never think to change the first drafts of tables and diagrams. ··· Three guiding principles should be
- the facts must be correct, but not exaggeratedly detailed in relation to purpose;
- the arrangements must be designed for easy comprehension by the reader, rather than for pleasure to the author;
- the information content should be high, relative to the total consumption of ink, and unnecessary distractions to eye and brain should be avoided.

Finney D J. 1986. On presenting tables and diagrams. *Journal of Scholarly Publishing* 17: 327–342

look for specific information: What is being said about whom? Why is this particular cell blank? What is the source of this information? How current is the information?

A style for tables should facilitate both stages, namely a quick overview and detailed scrutiny. The style should also take into account such practical problems as tables that are too wide, too tall, or too narrow; tables that have to be split across pages; and too many tables. This chapter follows the parts of a typical table in sequence, beginning from a sentence in text that mentions the table and ending with the first line of text after the break caused by the table.

Simple, open, or informal tables

Some tables are closely related to the text that precedes them and are not meant to stand on their own. Small and simple, consisting of only a few rows and usually only two columns, they are little more than lists in a slightly different form. Such tables are neither numbered, nor given a separate title, nor separated from the surrounding text with horizontal rules — and are not discussed further in this chapter.

Effective organization of data

Tables are compact and make efficient storage bins for data. However, the data often tell a story or support an argument, and the rows and columns should be effectively arranged for that purpose. Take the earlier example of a table showing the monthly average maximum temperature of four Indian cities: the 12 months form the rows, in chronological order, and the 4 cities form the columns, in alphabetic order, so that we get a tall and narrow table that fits well on an upright page. As a look-up table, this works well enough: given a city and the month, the temperature can be ascertained quickly. But what about the underlying patterns or highlights, if any? Which is the warmest city? Which is the warmest month? Which month shows the least variation across cities? Of the several possible ways in

> When reading a table of numbers we need to remember some or all of the numbers, at least momentarily. ⋯ This is easier with short numbers than with longer ones ⋯ Short-term memory and immediate recall are required in any mental arithmetic and even for just scanning a set of numbers. The fewer demands we make of our fragile short-term memories, the easier we find the task.
>
> Ehrenberg A S C. 1981. The problem of numeracy. *The American Statistician* **35**: 67–71

> On June 14, 1991, Leroy Burrell ran 100 meters in 9.90 seconds, establishing what was then a world record. But why 9.90? Why not spare some ink and write 9.9 instead? Because 9.90 tells us that Burrell's time was recorded in hundredths, and not tenths, of a second. A time of 9.90 does not equal 9.92 (the previous world record) or 9.86 (the subsequent world record), while 9.9 could equal either. The digits used to express a number's precision are collectively called 'significant digits' (or 'significant figures'). The number 9.90 has three significant digits; 9.9 has two.
>
> Niederman D and Boyum D. 2003. *What the Numbers Say: a field guide to mastering our numerical world*, pp. 75–76. New York: Broadway Books. 278 pp.

Handling numbers

which the table can be organized, we should choose the order that best supports the story or the argument—and it will be a rare coincidence if that order happens to be the alphabetical order or the order in which the data were recorded. Our hypothetical example may well be a part of a paper about the aggregate sales of air conditioners in the five cities, in which case we may consider averaging the temperatures across the cities and arranging the months in descending order of the average. Here are a few tips on presenting data in tabular form.

Order the rows or columns so that the order reflects the structure of the data As the British Standard puts it, 'The characteristic of a good table is that the main patterns and exceptions are self-evident' (British Standards Institution 1992).

Wherever appropriate, round off the values Use the least number of decimal places commensurate with the precision inherent in the data. Average yield of wheat – in tonnes per hectare, for instance – may well be given to only one place of the decimal whereas the maximum permissible limits of pesticide residues in drinking water require far greater precision.

Keep the numbers within a hundred (two effective digits) Appropriate choice of units (kilometres instead of metres, megawatts instead of kilowatts, etc.) makes this possible. Readers normally want to compare at least two values, which means that they need to hold both the values in their working memory simultaneously. And we can retain numbers in our immediate memory, despite interruptions, as long as the numbers are only two digits long (Simon 1969, cited in Ehrenberg 1981).

Referring to a table in continuous text

In most technical documents, tables are adjuncts to text, inserted mainly to supplement it. Keep the following tips in mind while writing the text that introduces one or more tables.
- Refer to the table by its number. Make sure that every table is numbered and referred to at least once in the text.

Chapter **6** Setting the table

> Example

The average maximum temperature, by month, for four Indian cities is given in Table 1; it shows that Ahmedabad, at 34.4 °C, is the warmest and Bangalore, at 29 °C, is the coolest.
  Offer a verbal summary of the table and highlight significant features, if any, as appropriate.

> Quote

> If a piece (report, paper, article, or whatever) has only one table, should it be referred to as Table 1?

A single table should not be numbered.

Editors of the Chicago Manual of Style
University of Chicago Press
[e-mail message dated 22 Feb. 2003]

However, if a document has only one table, do not number it; reference to 'the table' is adequate since there is only one.
- Tell the reader what the table is all about, mentioning its highlight, if any. This verbal summary of a table is particularly useful because it helps readers to quickly grasp the table's structure.
- Put the word 'Table', and the number that follows it, within parentheses if necessary, depending on the way the sentence is constructed.
- Always capitalize the word Table when it is followed by its number, as in 'In December, the average maximum temperature in Delhi is 22.8 °C (Table 1)'. Avoid such long-winded or ambiguous constructions as 'It can be seen in Table 1 that, in December, the average maximum temperature in Delhi is 22.8 °C.'
- If all the numbers in a table share the same unit (°C, for example, for the table mentioned at the beginning of this chapter), make sure that it is mentioned in the verbal summary.
- As far as possible, insert a table immediately after the paragraph in which it is mentioned.

Scheme for numbering tables

It is best to number all the tables (so long as there are two or more) within a document consecutively if the document is a homogeneous entity (a report or a book, for instance, in which different chapters are *not* attributed to different individuals). On the other hand, in publishing papers presented at a conference, for example, or in a book in which different chapters are written by different individuals, each paper or chapter is a different entity, in which case it is best to start numbering tables (and figures and appendixes, for that matter) afresh in each paper or chapter.

In some publications, both systems are combined by giving each table a number that consists of two numbers: the first number is that of the chapter and the second one is the serial

> **Example**
>
> ① ② ③ ④
>
> **Table 1** Average monthly maximum temperature (°C) in four Indian cities
>
> ⑤ ⑥
>
> 1 Use bold only for the word 'Table' and the number that follows it.
> 2 Skip the punctuation after the number.
> 3 Follow normal capitalization for the title.
> 4 Set the unit of measurement, if any, in bold.
> 5 Do not indent the second or subsequent lines in multi-line titles.
> 6 Skip the closing punctuation (unless the title is a complete sentence).

> **Quote** 
>
> Is the title satisfactory? Does it identify the table clearly and accurately?
>
> Does it contain unnecessary words? The title should not give background information, or duplicate the headings, or describe results. Normally, it will not even have a verb. It is purely descriptive.
>
> Is the title of this table consistent in style and form with titles of other tables in the series?
>
> Does the table title or subtitle (if there is one) give necessary information about units of measurement, size of sample, or methods of treatment? Does any such information refer to the *entire* table—to every column of data? If it doesn't, move the information to the appropriate column heading.
>
> Montagnes I. 1991. *Editing and Publication: a training manual*, p. 141. Manila: International Rice Research Institute. 429 pp.

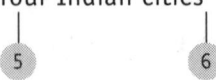

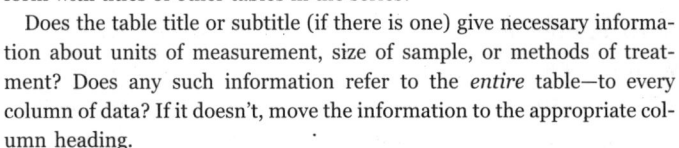

number of a table *within* that chapter. Table 1·7, for instance, means the 7th table in the first chapter; Table 4·2 means the 2nd table in the 4th chapter; and so on. Though the scheme makes it easier for editors to locate any table, and is more flexible in that tables can be added or taken out from individual chapters without much inconvenience, it can be puzzling to inexperienced readers when the first chapter contains no tables. The first table that readers would encounter within such a document may well be Table 3·1, for instance, making them wonder whether they have overlooked the earlier tables.

Use a separate numbering sequence for tables within appendixes or annexes attached to individual chapters or to the entire document: for instance, if Appendix A includes two tables, label them Table A·1 and Table A·2, and so on.

Mark 'part tables', that is, separate tables within a series, as Table 1a, Table 1b, and so on: for instance, '**Table 1a** Weather data for Delhi' and '**Table 1b** Weather data for Pune', etc.

Titles of tables

Each table must have both a number and a title: the number helps in locating the table and the title indicates concisely what the table contains. The following list covers in detail the many points of style related to table number and title.

- Use bold only for the word Table and the number that follows it.
- Avoid any punctuation mark between the table number and the table title.
- Begin the title with a capital letter; thereafter, use capitals as you would normally use them in any continuous text—do not capitalize every word.
- Make units of measurement a part of the title so long as they apply to the entire table. Insert the units immediately after the word to which they refer, enclose them in parentheses, and highlight them by making them bold, as in '**Table 7** Consumption of coal (**million tonnes**) in different sectors'.
- The title is rarely a complete sentence: do not end it with a full stop.

Chapter **6** Setting the table

Table 3 World imports and exports of petroleum products: 1990 to 1999

Supply the year/s to which the data refer to, if appropriate.

Example

Table 1 Average monthly maximum temperature (°C) in three Indian cities

Month	Ahmedabad	Bangalore	Hyderabad
January	28.4	27.0	28.6
February	31.3	29.6	31.8
March	36.0	32.4	35.2
April	39.9	33.6	37.6
May	41.8	32.7	38.8
June	38.4	29.2	34.4
July	33.3	27.5	30.5
August	31.9	27.4	29.6
September	33.4	28.0	30.1
October	35.8	27.7	30.4
November	33.2	26.6	28.8
December	29.8	25.9	27.8

Example

Use the normal page-width for the title; the table itself may be narrower.

Table 1 Average monthly maximum temperature (°C) in Ahmedabad, Bangalore, and Hyderabad

Month	Ahmedabad	Bangalore	Hyderabad
January	28.4	27.0	28.6
February	31.3	29.6	31.8
March	36.0	32.4	35.2
April	39.9	33.6	37.6
May	41.8	32.7	38.8
June	38.4	29.2	34.4

Example

If the title runs to two or more lines, do not indent the additional lines.

Table 1 Average monthly maximum temperature (°C) in Ahmedabad, Bangalore, and Hyderabad

[Observations recorded at 08:30 and 17:30 hours Indian Standard Time]

Month	Ahmedabad	Bangalore	Hyderabad
January	28.4	27.0	28.6
February	31.3	29.6	31.8
March	36.0	32.4	35.2
April	39.9	33.6	37.6
May	41.8	32.7	38.8
June	38.4	29.2	34.4

Example

Place notes that apply to the whole table as a headnote, between the title and the body of the table.

- If the table gives data for a given period, mention that period specifically at the end of the title.
- Let the title run to the normal width of a page: do not try to match its width to the width of the table.
- If the title runs to the next line (or longer), do not indent the second and the subsequent lines; each such line begins directly underneath the 'T' of Table.
- Always set table titles left-justified no matter what justification is followed for the accompanying text.

General note/s to a table

A table title needs to be short so that it conveys at a glance what the table is all about. However, if you wish to qualify that title in some way or to offer more information about the table as a whole, put such information in the form of a note placed *after* the title but *before* the body of the table. Put the entire note within square brackets and use the same font as that used for the table. Do not label this text as Note or Notes. If more than one, use a bullet for each of the notes.

Column heads

Typically, a table consists of columns and rows, each with a heading of its own. All the row heads together, which make up the column at extreme left, are sometimes referred to as 'stub', and their heading indicates what is common to all the rows. For example, in the table showing the maximum and minimum temperatures, the stub heading would be Month. Stub headings may be singular or plural; in this example the heading is singular because it refers to each of the months in turn. Always give an appropriate and informative heading in this cell; never leave it blank. Set this heading in normal type, neither italics nor bold.

Set all the other column heads in italics *except* units of measurement, which are always set in normal type, as in *Temperature* (°C) or *Weight* (kg). If column heads consist solely of scientific names of plants or animals, set them in italics. However, if the names are only a part of the heading, set the names in normal type and the rest of the text in italics.

Chapter **6** Setting the table

Month	Ahmed-abad	Bangalore	Hyder-abad	New Delhi Safdar-jang	Palam
January	28.4	27.0	28.6	21.1	21.0
February	31.3	29.6	31.8	24.2	24.1
March	36.0	32.4	35.2	30.0	30.2

Example

If column headings run to two or more lines, align them at the base.

				New Delhi	
Month	Ahmed-abad	Bangalore	Hyder-abad	Safdar-jang	Palam
January	28.4	27.0	28.6	21.1	21.0
February	31.3	29.6	31.8	24.2	24.1
March	36.0	32.4	35.2	30.0	30.2

Example

Use a spanner rule to group subheadings within a column heading.

Column headings

If numerical multipliers are used, spell out the multiplier in words, as in *Population* (in millions) or *Households* (in thousands): *do not* use a series of zeros with an apostrophe stuck at the beginning, as in ('ooo).

When space is limited, abbreviations are acceptable in column heads so long as they are self-explanatory. If a column heading is too long, abbreviate it and explain the abbreviation in a footnote.

If some column heads run to more than one line, align them from the bottom; this eliminates the gap between the body and the head of a column.

Some column heads may have subheads or be divided into more than two levels. To continue the example given at the beginning of this chapter, temperatures may be recorded at more than one point within a city, and these points then form subheads. For example, for Mumbai, the table may give the temperatures recorded at both Colaba and Santa Cruz and for Delhi, the figures for both Palam and Safdarjang may be supplied. This makes it necessary to use what are referred to as 'spanner' or 'straddle' rules, that is, horizontal lines that span all the subheadings within a heading. In this example, Delhi is centred on the horizontal line that encompasses Safdarjang and Palam. If several levels of headings occur within column heads, a more elaborate typographic arrangement may be required.

Break a long column heading into two or more lines if necessary to prevent the column from becoming too wide. As far as possible, introduce the breaks logically so as to facilitate comprehension.

Column headings can be right aligned, centred, or left aligned, depending on the alignment used for the body of the column. In most tables that present numerical data, the columns are right aligned if they comprise only whole numbers (integers) and aligned by the decimal point if the data are presented in decimal numbers. In both cases, set the column head aligned to the right. If a column is left aligned (for reasons explained below), its head is also set left aligned.

Table 7 Environmental indicators of selected countries

Indicator	China	Egypt	India	Sweden
Forest area as a percentage of total land area (%)	17.5	0.1	21.6	65.9
Annual withdrawal of fresh water (billion cubic metres)	526	55	500	3
Emissions of organic water pollutants (tonnes/day)	8492	226	1760	91
Emissions of carbon dioxide per capita (tonnes)	16.6	2.0	1.1	5.5

Left-align the entries in a column if they do not share the same unit.

✗

Table 7 Environmental indicators of selected countries

Indicator	Unit
Forest area as a percentage of total land area	%
Annual withdrawal of fresh water	billion cubic metres
Emissions of organic water pollutants	tonnes/day
Emissions of carbon dioxide per capita	tonnes

✓

Table 7 Environmental indicators of selected countries

Indicator
Forest area as a percentage of total land area (%)
Annual withdrawal of fresh water (billion cubic metres)
Emissions of organic water pollutants (tonnes/day)
Emissions of carbon dioxide per capita (tonnes)

The variable and the unit go together; do not put the units in a separate column.

Body of the column

Whenever all entries within a column share the same unit – temperature, weight, length, or whatever – the column is set either right aligned or decimal aligned. However, when all entries within a column do not share a common unit, they are set left aligned. For instance, take a table that compares half a dozen countries, each forming one column, on the basis of such parameters as geographical area, population, gross domestic product, length of coastline, and total exports. Each parameter occupies a row. Therefore, within a single column, one cell would show the population (say in millions), another would show the area (say in million square kilometres), and so on. Each of these numbers is expressed in a different unit of measurement. In this case, the entries are always left aligned.

Row headings

Row headings typically occupy the left-most column in a table. Whereas spanner rules are used to indicate levels of headings for columns, indenting is the most commonly used device to mark subheadings within a row heading: a subheading begins a little farther away to the right than the main heading; a sub-subheading begins even farther; and so on. However, this system has its limitations because by intruding into the body of the table it can end up taking a great deal of valuable space. In the earlier example of a table that compares different countries, do not assign a separate column for the disparate units: the variable and the unit go together, within the same cell, but separated with a comma (as in Length of coastline, km or Population, in millions).

Horizontal alignment within a row

At times, the row heading in the extreme left column may run to more than one line whereas all other cells within that row occupy only one line. In such cases, all the entries will align with the *last* line of the row heading when all of them are in the

Table 7 Proved reserves (**trillion cubic metres**) of natural gas

Region	1982	1992	2002
North America	10.67	9.45	7.15
South and Central America	3.14	5.34	7.08
Europe and Eurasia	39.96	61.02	61.04
Middle East	21.78	43.05	56.06
Africa	5.36	9.82	11.84
Asia Pacific	4.99	9.66	12.61

If row heads run to two lines or more, align the numbers in that row with the *last* line of the row heading.

If a table consists of text, align the entries in the body a row with the *top* line of the row heading.

form of numbers. If the cells mostly contain text, their contents will align with the *first* line of the row heading.

Notation for missing values

Do not leave any cell of a table blank lest the reader should wonder whether it is an oversight. Use the following symbols consistently: (a) a question mark in square brackets [?] for 'not available'; (b) an em dash (—) for 'not applicable'; and (c) two dots for 'negligible' (when the values are too small to matter).

These symbols are recommended because they are more or less self-explanatory. However, do not leave readers guessing. In a document that has many tables in which these symbols are used, the notation can be explained in an introductory note or included along with a list of abbreviations.

Footnotes

Whereas general notes refer to the entire table, footnotes direct a reader's attention to specific cells within a table. This is useful to highlight any departure from normal. For example, in a table that shows the monthly maximum and minimum temperatures in five cities, most values may be based on a 30-year average. However, the values for only one city may be based on a 10-year average. In that case, a footnote mark is placed next to the name of that city and the footnote itself supplies the necessary qualification. Footnotes are also used to expand the abbreviations used within a table.

Here are some points of style relevant to footnotes within a table.

Choice of footnote markers Use letters of the alphabet as markers. Superscript numbers are common but they are best used within tables that contain text instead of numerical information. With numerical information, it is safer to use letters of the alphabet. Avoid using such symbols as octothorps (#) and pilcrows (¶). However, it is common to use asterisks to indicate the level of statistical significance (one star for a probability level of 0.1%, two for a level of 0.05%, and three for 0.01%).

Use alphabets as footnote markers and assign them in the normal reading sequence, left to right, moving downwards.

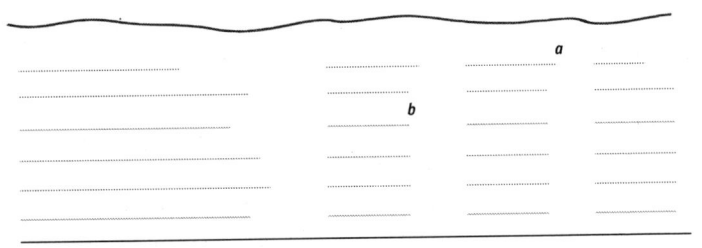

✗ *a* Provisional *b* Final

✓ *a* provisional *b* final

Avoid starting a footnote with a capital letter.

Footnotes: format, placement, and sequence

Format for markers To make the markers prominent, present them as superscripts, make them bold, and set them in italics.

Placement of markers Watch for any misalignment caused by footnote markers. Traditionally, a footnote marker is placed *after* the item that it marks. Because of that, when all the entries within a column of numbers are aligned to the right, the number with a footnote marker is forced farther to the left, making it out of alignment with other numbers. To prevent this, insert the marker *before* the item whenever all other items are right aligned.

Sequence of markers Assign the markers in the same order in which normal text is read, that is, in successive sweeps from left to right while moving from the top to the bottom. For example, if two items within the same row are to be marked 'a' and 'b', the one to the left is assigned the letter 'a'. Similarly, if two items within the same column are to be assigned these letters, the one in the higher row is assigned the letter 'a'.

Explaining footnotes Footnotes to a table are placed immediately after the table and not at the foot of the page on which the table appears. The marker appears first, in a format identical to its counterpart within the table (bold, superscript, and italics), and the explanation follows immediately, without any gap. Avoid starting the explanation with a capital letter as far as possible; it makes the superscripted footnote marker less prominent. If this cannot be avoided, insert a non-breaking space between the marker and the capital letter.

Source/s

Supply complete details about the source, if any, of the information presented in a table right down to the number of the page on which the source appears in the original document. If the entire table is reproduced from another source, written permission to reproduce that table must be obtained from whomsoever holds the copyright to that source. (The copyright holder may not necessarily be the author but it is courteous to seek the author's permission—some publishers require it before granting the permission to reproduce tables or figures.)

Chapter **6** Setting the table

Example

SOURCE _____

The word 'Source' is followed by the bibliographic details (or web address) of the source on the same line.

SOURCES
1/ _____
2/ _____
3/ _____

The word 'Sources' gets a line to itself; the details (or web address) of each source are given in the form of a numbered list.

Quote

··· one test of tables is whether or not they can be read out loud. This is a test that particularly the editor has to perform—the writer is too close to the material and therefore not objective enough. What I mean by reading the table out loud is picking at random any cell and saying out loud what it tells you, e.g. 'The average temperature in Delhi in February is 17 degrees Celsius.' Simple. You would be surprised ··· how many tables look really nice but are virtually unreadable because the headings are not descriptive enough.
    Lynn P Nygaard
    Information Officer, CICERO (Center for International Climate and Environment Research at Oslo)
    [e-mail message dated 27 Feb. 2002]

The format for citing the source document is the same as that explained in Chapter 8. A few pointers to the recommended style are given in the following list.

- Use 'Source' or 'Sources' as appropriate as the heading for the bibliographic information. Set the word in capital letters.
- If there is only one source, insert a space after the word 'Source' and continue with the bibliographic information, starting from the author/s, followed by the year of publication, as in Gupta 1998 or TERI 1999.
- If the heading is 'Sources', leave the rest of the line blank and supply the bibliographic information as a numbered list.
- If a table is constructed from somebody else's data, indicate that fact by adding 'Data from' before the reference, as in Data from Jones 1998. Likewise, use 'Adapted from' before the reference to indicate that the form of the table differs from that in the cited source. (See also p. 116.)

Table design and format

Make tables compact: it is not necessary for every table to be as wide as the text block. Set the columns of a table fairly close (a gap of 3 to 5 mm on either side is sufficient) and make each column only as wide as necessary to accommodate the widest cell. If necessary, split a wide column head into more than one line. A few other points of format and design are listed below.

Make tables uncluttered: it is not necessary to separate adjacent columns with vertical rules and adjacent rows with horizontal rules—a table is an orderly arrangement of columns and rows, not a collection of boxes. Vertical rules are seldom necessary; in fact, they are an obstacle to scanning. And three horizontal rules are usually adequate: one at the top, between the title of table and the table itself; one near the top, between the column heads and the body of the table; and one at the bottom, between the body of the table and the rest (footnotes and source notes, if any). The horizontal rule that separates column heads from the body of the table should be less

> A second source of difficulty for readers can arise from another standard publishing policy—that of making tables and figures fit the standard width of the columns of print (either single, double, or treble). Such a policy results from a need to 'balance' the page artistically rather than from a proper consideration of the reader's needs. Fitting a table into a particular column width can cause difficulties if there is too much or too little data, and such difficulties can be increased if the resulting intercolumn spacing is inappropriate.
> Hartley J. 1991. Tabling information. *American Psychologist* 46: 655–656

Avoid vertical lines in a table; three horizontal lines are usually adequate.

abcdef

ghijklm

A complex table may require additional horizontal lines.

conspicuous than the other two. If these are 1-point thick, for instance, make the middle rule half a point thick.

Positioning tables within text pages

Given that tables do not come in fixed sizes, it is not practical to lay down rigid rules about how they should be placed on text pages. The suggestions that follow are aimed at making it easier for the reader to locate tables and to use them effectively in combination with the accompanying text.

As mentioned before, the best position for a table is immediately after the paragraph in which the table is mentioned. However, this is not always possible: (a) the end of the paragraph may mark the end of the page itself, with no room for a table; (b) a paragraph may mention a figure and a table, only one of which can be fitted into the available space; or (c) the table may be so broad that it has to be printed in the 'landscape' format.

The next best choice is to place the table on the same page on which the table is mentioned, even when it means placing the table *before* the text that refers to it. The third option is to place the text that mentions a table and the table itself within the *same page spread* (two pages that face each other when a document is open). If none of these three will do, place the table as near as possible after the text that mentions it.

If a table occupies *almost* all the page, fill the rest of the page with a block of continuous text so long as the block is at least 4 lines long—if the page has space only for 3 or fewer lines, leave that space blank.

If a table occupies *less* than half a page, it can be placed between two text blocks; if it is only slightly larger, place it either at the top of a page, with text below, or the other way around, with text above.

Landscape tables

The discussion so far relates to 'portrait' or upright or tall tables that appear in one piece on a typical page. 'Landscape'

Position a small table between blocks of text. Place a table that fills half a page or more either above or below the text block.

Place tables printed sideways on a page ('landscape' tables) such that the table title is flush with the left margin of a page. If the table is wide but short, it may have some blank space at the foot.

tables are those that are wider than they are tall and are printed sideways on a page.

When turned sideways, the top of the table abuts the left margin. In other words, the left margin becomes the top margin and the top margin becomes the right margin. If the table is wide enough, it will fill all the space between the bottom and top margins of the ordinary upright page; if deep enough, it will also extend up to the right margin of the ordinary page. If the table is not deep enough, some blank space will be left between the table and the right margin. If the table is not so wide, centre it on the page so that the blank space to its right and left is the same.

Tables split across more than one page

Some tables are too long (too many rows) to fit within a single page; others are so wide (too many columns or very wide columns) that they cannot fit within a page even after printing them sideways (in landscape mode). Such tables have to be split, which at once raises some more issues of style, described below.

The 'Continued' line

Place the '*Continued*' line immediately below and to the right of the block that contains the top part of a split. The form is to omit the table number and to set the line in italics, with a capital 'C'.

On the next page, the first line, set indented, reads '*Table x continued*'; the column headings are repeated; and the table continues with the row that follows the row on the previous page. This sequence (with '*Continued*' line at foot) is repeated on each fresh page until the table is complete. Footnotes and source notes follow next.

Dispense with the '*Continued*' line in a landscape table fitted within a page-spread if the whole table is visible at the same time when the document is turned sideways.

Print *'Continued'* at bottom right to indicate that the table continues on the next page. Print *'Table x continued'* at top left. Repeat column headings. The table may continue across several pages.

Do not repeat column headings in a landscape table laid out across a page-spread.

Large tables that cannot fit within a normal page

Tables that are simply too large to fit within a page require special handling. Printing them in very small type (smaller than 7 points, as a rule of thumb) makes it hard to read them easily or accurately and virtually impossible to read as a photocopy. Provided such tables are few, one solution is to print them on larger sheets and fold them in, a time-consuming operation. If such tables are many, you may want to consider printing the entire document in a large size or issuing the tables as a supplementary volume. Large tables can also be made available on a permanent web site or as spreadsheet files (Excel, QuattroPro, etc.) on a disk.

References

British Standards Institution. 1992
BS 7581: 1992. Guide to presentation of tables and graphs
London: British Standards Institution.

Ehrenberg A S C. 1981
The problem of numeracy
The American Statistician 35 (2): 67–71

*Simon H A. 1969
The Sciences of the Artificial
Cambridge, Massachusetts, USA: MIT Press. 123 pp.
[Karl Taylor Compton Lectures, 1968]

*cited in Ehrenberg 1981

Chapter 7 at a glance

When to use illustrations
Types of illustrations
Charts and graphs
Size and proportion
Style for labels, axes, legends, etc.
Photographs and 35-millimetre slides
 Things to avoid in a photograph
 Handling photographs for print production
Scanning for printing and for display on screen
 Illustrations in electronic form for printing
Integrating illustrations with text
Bibliography

7 ▶ Figures of speech

charts, diagrams, maps, photographs

There is only so much that text or tabular information can do: illustrations are far more efficient in displaying complex structures, patterns rich in details, marked trends in a series of numbers, and so on.

However, if they are to do their job well, figures have to be crafted with some care. This chapter answers a few commonly asked questions, including the following.
▶ What is a good size for an illustration?
▶ What is a suitable resolution for scanning?
▶ How should different parts of a diagram be labelled?
▶ Why are charts often prepared twice as large as the final size?
▶ When is it better to use a table instead of a chart?

The chapter begins with some thoughts on when, that is in what situations, to use illustrations and what purpose they serve, and then goes on to describe different types of illustrations – particularly charts – and the points of style associated with each. The chapter concludes with some advice on handling illustrations during the publication process and some guidance on labelling and packing them if they are to accompany a manuscript being submitted for publication elsewhere. Illustrations, as used here, include charts and graphs (either on paper or prepared in electronic form), photographs and 35-mm slides (again, on paper or film or in digital format), drawings prepared in such packages as CorelDraw, and so on.

When to use illustrations

Now that computers make it possible for many writers to try their hand at being illustrators as well, you will find yourself concentrating not so much on whether to include illustrations as on how to combine them with text to the best advantage.

> Excellence in statistical graphics consists of complex ideas communicated with clarity, precision, and efficiency. Graphical displays should
> - show the data
> - induce the viewer to think about the substance rather than about methodology, graphic design, the technology of graphic production, or something else
> - avoid distorting what the data have to say
> - present many numbers in a small space
> - make large data sets coherent
> - encourage the eye to compare different pieces of data
> - reveal the data at several levels of detail, from a broad overview to the fine structure
> - serve a reasonably clear purpose: description, exploration, tabulation, or decoration
> - be closely integrated with the statistical and verbal descriptions of a data set.
>
> Tufte E R. 1983. *The Visual Display of Quantitative Information*, p. 13. Cheshire, Connecticut, USA: Graphics Press. 197 pp.

REACHING OUT TO WOMEN WITH VISUAL MATERIAL
A Designer's Experience

Ms. Lakshmi Murthy, a designer, gives us an insight into the complexity of providing posters for people who lack formal education.

BACKGROUND: A health message pasted on an Indian village wall showed these two pots:

Rodhi Bai, who belonged to this village saw the poster and interpreted it in the following way.

Drawing A: there is a pot behind two bamboo sticks. There are house flies on the mouth of the pot.

Drawing B: the pot has a lid and there is a symbol next to it.

Rhodi Bai, like thousands of Indian women and others on the subcontinent has never been to school. To her symbols like A and B have no meaning at all.

Drawing A

Drawing B

Source *Views: a newsletter on gender* (Winter 1995): p. 2
[published from Bangalore, India]

Functions of illustrations

Maps, technical drawings of physical objects, flowcharts that illustrate a process, photographs of people, and charts that show numerical data at a glance are just some examples of illustrations that are essential, where they fulfil a function that text simply cannot serve. But illustrations are useful in other ways too, because they

- break up the text and thus make it appear more inviting
- convey the tone of the book – serious reading or light reading, for specialists or for the general reader, in-depth treatment or a quick overview – to someone who is simply leafing through the document
- make a statement about the document: full-colour photographs suggest a lavish and prestigious production; detailed, precisely drawn illustrations suggest a technical approach; cartoons suggest lighter reading; and so on
- help readers by providing faster access to information
- provide evidence, for example photographs of microscopic structures
- add to the background information, for example pictures of locations
- often serve a different segment of readers, namely those who are more accustomed to thinking in visual terms: engineers, cartographers, graphic designers, and even children.

Therefore, you may want to consider including illustrations even when they are not strictly necessary.

Types of illustrations

Illustrations can be classified in many ways but, keeping in mind the way they are reproduced, they fall into two simple categories: line and tone. Line illustrations are those in which image areas and non-image areas are clearly differentiated: any point on a sheet of paper, or a pixel on a screen, is either marked (and thus carries a part of the image) or unmarked (blank) — there are no shades of grey. Lines, shapes (circles, filled or empty; boxes, stars, arrows, etc.), and even text can all

Table 1 Monthly rainfall (**mm**) in three Indian cities

Month	Mumbai	Srinagar	Trivandrum
Jan.	2.0	72.8	20.1
Feb.	1.1	72.3	20.3
Mar.	0.4	104.1	43.5
Apr.	2.8	78.1	122.1
May	16.0	63.4	248.6
June	520.3	35.6	331.2
July	709.5	61.0	215.4
Aug.	439.3	62.8	164.0
Sept.	297.0	31.8	122.9
Oct.	88.0	28.7	271.2
Nov.	20.6	17.5	206.9
Dec.	2.2	35.9	73.1

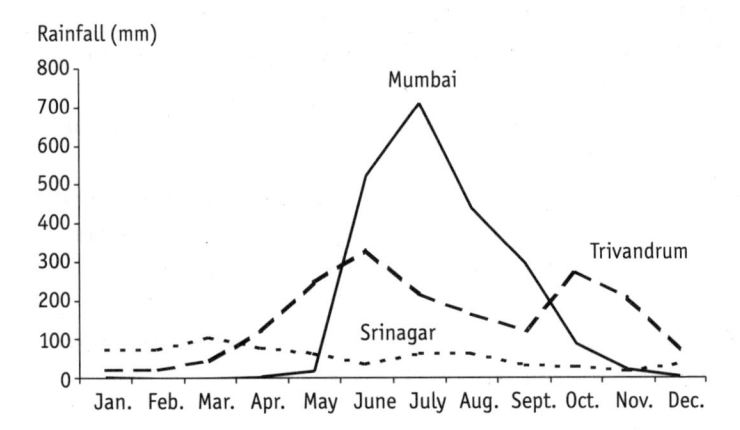

Figure 1 Monthly rainfall (mm) in three Indian cities

> Graphs are usually more effective in communicating broad differences (e.g. large or small) than in conveying specific quantities (e.g. the precise size of a section of a pie chart or the slope or a trend line). If it is difficult to convey specific data without showing numbers on the graph, or, if there are many numbers, a well laid-out table is likely to convey them more clearly than a graph.
>   BSI. 1992. *Guide to presentation of tables and graphs*, p. 11. London: British Standards Institution. 24 pp. [BS 7581: 1992]

be grouped as line illustrations. Commonly used charts and graphs fall in the same category. Line illustrations are easy to handle and can easily be photocopied. They reproduce fairly cleanly even at low resolutions (150 dpi). TIFF (tag image file format) files typically contain line illustrations.

Tone illustrations are those that use shades of colour (or shades of grey in black-and-white illustrations): they may have lines or patches that are neither black nor white but of some intermediate colour, pastel shades, and so on.

Paintings, photographs of people and places, of plants and animals, etc. are typical examples of this category of images. Such images are far more difficult to reproduce—even at 600 dpi, the reproduction is poor; most photocopiers cannot handle these at all: the shades of grey disappear, coming out as either white or dense black. When scanned, the files are generally large. JPEG (joint photographic expert group) files are typically of tone illustrations.

Charts and graphs

Charts that represent data pictorially are the most common type of illustrations used in technical documents. Such charts enable readers to take in the data at a glance and convey the message almost instantaneously. Therefore, use them to show a trend or to show comparisons: if actual numbers are important and detailed information has to be given, the data are best shown in a table. Compare the information presented in Table 1 and Figure 1. Though both present the same data, Figure 1 shows at a glance the distinctive patterns of the *distribution* of annual rainfall—something that only a close analysis of Table 1 will reveal.

However, if what is important is not the distribution but the total amount of rainfall, you need to use another type of chart, namely a bar chart in this case (Figure 2). And if the idea is not so much to compare different places as different seasons, a pie chart (Figure 3) is what you need.

Therefore, you need to decide what it is that the illustration should highlight and then choose the type of chart – line, bar,

Annual rainfall (mm)

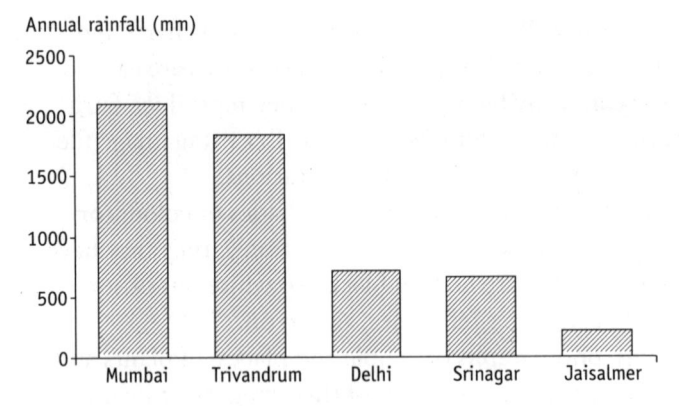

[Bar chart showing annual rainfall: Mumbai ~2100, Trivandrum ~1850, Delhi ~720, Srinagar ~680, Jaisalmer ~220]

Figure 2 Annual rainfall in five cities

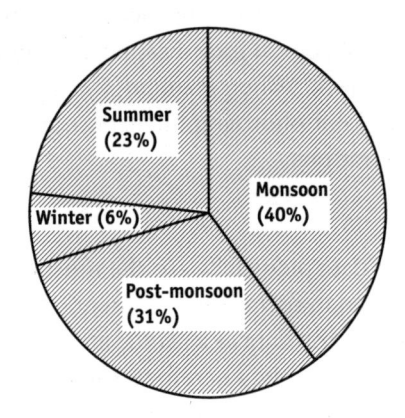

[Pie chart showing seasonal distribution: Summer (23%), Monsoon (40%), Post-monsoon (31%), Winter (6%)]

Figure 3 Seasonal distribution of annual rainfall in Trivandrum (total rainfall = 1790 mm)

| Address | www.eia.doe.gov/neic/graphs/preface.htm |

Quote

Before constructing a statistical graph, an author should make two decisions. The first decision is to determine what the message is that the graph will communicate (or the purpose). The second decision is closely related to the first. The author needs to decide who the audience is and what they will expect or extract from the graph. When these decisions are made, the question of format and design can be answered. ⋯ Thus, the fundamental task in designing a statistical graph is to focus readers' attention on the graph's data and its message, not on its design.

 Rutchik R H. 1999. EIA guidelines for statistical graphs. Energy Information Administration, Washington, DC.

pie, percentage bar, area, etc. – accordingly. A style manual can offer little help in making that choice; however, once you have made the choice, the following notes can help you design and label the chart more effectively.

Size and proportion

What is a good size for a chart? How large or small should it be? The answers can be straightforward if you know the publication in which the chart is to appear because it is the size of the publication that governs the size of the illustration: it should fit within the print area of a single page or, if essential, within two facing pages. Take project reports, for example: typically, they are produced on A4 sheets (21 cm wide and 29.7 cm tall). Taking the right and left margins as 2.5 cm each, a figure cannot be wider than 16 cm nor, taking into account the top and bottom margins, taller than 24.7 cm. At a pinch, the height could stretch a little more if we omit page headers and footers for that page. However, these dimensions are the upper limits: they tell us that the illustration cannot be wider or taller than the specified size but do not tell us what the optimum size should be. Many considerations, both practical and theoretical, influence the optimum size, a few of which are listed below in the form of suggestions for figures to be published in books, journals, etc.

▸ Make sure that even the smallest detail is clearly visible and that all the lettering is easy to read. A font size of 8 points is the smallest that you could possibly use. As a rule of thumb, the small 'x' of the font used should be at least 2 mm tall. For any lettering within a figure, try to use a font that is roughly the same size as that used for text. Avoid obtrusively large or bold lettering.
▸ Make even the thinnest line at least half a point thick.
▸ Leave a gap of at least half a millimetre between adjacent lines or dots used as a pattern.
▸ Use the font size used for the text as the upper limit for any lettering within the figure.

From: Laurence Penney <···>
Date: 1 March 2000
Subject: Captions: above or below?

In general, it is good practice and polite to introduce things before shoving them in the reader's face. Tables, like sections in a book, particularly need an introduction since they are symbolic—language and numbers abstracted away from their subject. A glance through a table is even less profitable than a glance through a block of text of that size. So tables need an introduction, hence a caption above them.

By contrast figures and pictures usually serve as their own introduction. They are analogous to what they represent, there's no change of mode. So it could be a tiny bit patronizing to 'introduce' them, more respectful to use a caption below, which does not demand to be read. There's another aspect to figures, if they are pictures – photos and drawings of life – rather than diagrams. They're typically darker towards the bottom, thanks first to gravity (dirt sinks, and things are bulkier the lower they get) and second to the sun and light bulbs (implying shadows). Thus we are used to muck and irrelevance at the bottom of our visual field, and are easily able to filter them out to appreciate the picture well. Odd items floating above the main subject are distracting, like aeroplanes, UFOs, or mosquitoes.

▸ In documents that use multiple columns, size the charts in 1-column increments: in other words, see if a chart can fit within a single column to begin with; if it does not, make it large enough so that fills two columns, and so on.

▸ Keep the overall proportions of a chart consistent with the page frame: 'tall' or 'portrait' mode in most cases but 'wide' or 'landscape' if the document is in that format or if otherwise necessary.

Style for labels, axes, legends, etc.

The two major objectives of a consistent style for graphics are (1) to make it easy for readers to extract all relevant information from a figure and (2) to make all figures within a document fit in harmoniously with the text. Choosing fonts that complement each other, placing labels and legends appropriately, choosing fill patterns within component bar charts, displaying the units of measurement—all these and more go into the making of effective graphics. The specimen charts included in this chapter show the recommended style described here.

Label for vertical axis Place the label on the top of the vertical axis, left-aligned with the numbers that mark off major divisions of the axis. The label reads horizontally; do not place it sideways and never stack it so that it reads from top to bottom with letters placed one below the other. If another variable is shown on another vertical axis, the label could be right aligned with the numbers on that axis.

Label for horizontal axis Place the label below the axis and parallel to it, centred on the length of the axis.

Labels for data lines, bars, segments, etc. As far as possible, label each line directly instead of preparing a separate key explaining the labels. The label runs horizontally; do not place it at an angle to follow the curve of the data line. Label each data line unambiguously. The same applies to bar charts. For segmented bar charts, label all the segments in the bar to the extreme right. With pie charts, put the labels within the segments only if you can do that with all segments; if not, arrange them to the

> To identify the values, use either a scale at the top (sometimes at the bottom) or numbers at the ends of the bars, not both. Use the scale if all you want is a fast study of the relationships; use the numbers if they are important to your message. At times, it's a good idea to use the scale and the one number that needs emphasis. Using both scale and numbers, however, is redundant and adds clutter to the bar chart, as it does, for that matter, to the column chart and the line chart.
>
> Zelazny G. 2001. *Say It With Charts: the executive's guide to visual communication*, 4th edn, p. 34. New York: McGraw-Hill. 226 pp.

> Furthermore, 3-D graphs are often prepared on PCs in multiple colours, and these then get transformed into black and white — with a consequent loss of clarity — when they are printed in books and journals. Authors need to be aware of this, and to take appropriate steps.
>
> Hartley J. 2001. Referees are not always right! The case of the 3-D graph. *British Journal of Educational Technology* **32**: 623–626

> The eye notices more change in the black-and-white spectrum between 20% and 30% than between 70% and 80%. ··· It's easy to specify screen densities on the desktop: 80% is very dark and 20% is quite light. People can't discern more than about five values of grey in the same frame.
>
> Rabb M Y. 1993. *The Presentation Design Book*, 2nd edn, pp. 136–137. Chapel Hill, North Carolina, USA: Ventana Press. 346 pp.

right and left of the pie and connect each segment to its label with a thin line. Make the percentage a part of the label.

Thickness of lines Just as we maintain a hierarchy of headings, so should we maintain a hierarchy of lines. In line charts, make the data lines the thickest; the axes of intermediate thickness; and the tick marks the thinnest. In pie charts and segmented bar charts, make the outline of the circle or of individual bars the thickest; the lines that divide the circle or the bar of intermediate thickness; and the lines that connect the segments to their labels the thinnest.

Gaps between bars Make sure that individual bars are wider than the gaps that separate one bar from the next.

Fill patterns and line patterns The patterns used as fills can have unexpected consequences. For instance, grey shades disappear during photocopying; very fine patterns consisting of lines spaced close together may turn into black patches if the image is reduced; and patterns consisting of vertical and horizontal lines placed next to each other can cause optical illusions: one segment may appear crooked or the bar may look pinched at the joint between the two patterns.

Shades of grey are useful so long as the diagrams are not likely to be photocopied. Shading is specified in terms of percentage: 100% is totally black and 0% is totally white. However, shades of less than 15% are difficult to reproduce and anything above 80% is perceived as totally black—it is best to confine the values to 20%, 40%, and 60%. With the addition of totally white and totally black, this system provides five clearly distinguishable groups.

Patterns are safer than shades especially if the figures are to be photocopied. Recommended patterns are small dots placed close together and large dots placed wider apart, cross-hatching, small squares placed closer and large squares placed wider, total black, and total white (blank). These patterns are stable and can withstand photocopying, reduction, and less-than-perfect printing quite well (Figure 4).

Chapter 7 Figures of speech

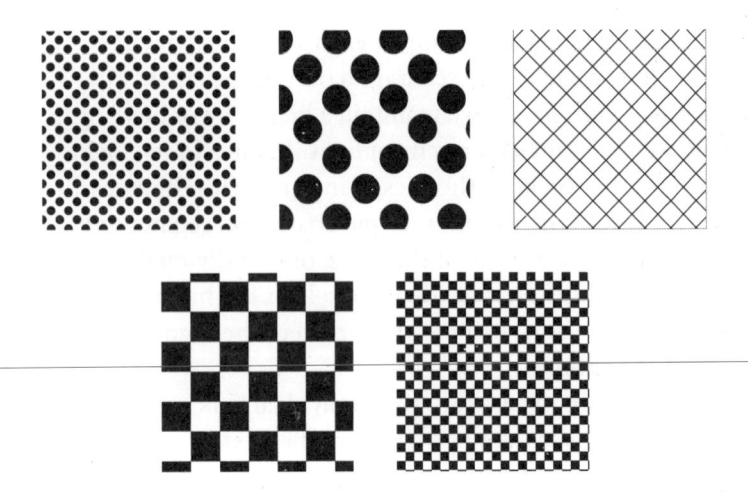

Figure 4 Recommended fill patterns for black-and-white illustrations

··· those templates served a very important purpose: to keep our charts simple. Computer graphics make it too easy go get fancy. The Firm uses charts as a means of expressing information in a readily understandable form. The simpler things are, the easier they are to understand. Therefore, McKinsey prints its charts in black and white; it avoids three-dimensional graphics unless absolutely necessary to convey the message; and it adheres to the cardinal rule of one message per chart.
Rasiel E M. 1999. *The McKinsey Way: using the techniques of the world's top strategic consultants to help you and your business*, p. 114. New York: McGraw-Hill. 188 pp.

Problems with 3-D graphs

If it is necessary to distinguish between lines, the choices are a solid line, a line consisting of long dashes, a line consisting of large dots, and a line in which dashes alternate with dots. Such patterns are better than using lines of different thickness.

Avoid three-dimensional graphs: they can introduce distortions. To make a pie chart appear solid, the circle is often stretched into an ellipse; a segment along the longer axis then appears larger than that along the shorter axis. In bar charts, it is difficult to tell the correct top edge: is it the one nearer to the reader or the one farther away? Adding the extra dimension also magnifies the differences between values because viewers take in the area (or, in the case of 3-D graphs, the volume) of a bar instead of its height, which is misleading.

Labels and leader lines Labels that identify parts of a diagram consist of text and lines, the leader lines, that connect the text to the appropriate part. Make the leader lines at least 6 mm long but avoid making them longer than 45 mm. Leave a gap of 1–2 mm between the text of the label and the tip of the leader line. Keep the text of labels short (four lines or fewer).

Photographs and 35-millimetre slides

Whereas charts and graphs are 'line' illustrations, photographs are 'tone' illustrations, consisting not merely of many colours but also of many shades of each colour. Even black-and-white photographs consist of not just black and white areas but of many shades of grey. The demands such images make on the process of reproducing them on paper or on screen are, therefore, more exacting than those made by 'line art' or simple text.

To start with, it is next to impossible to include photographs if the original is to be reproduced by photocopying using an ordinary photocopier. Better results are obtained if a special screen is placed between the glass surface of the photocopier and the photograph.

To print a few copies, it is better to scan the photographs, integrate them with text, and print the document on a colour printer. Currently (September 2003), this is an expensive option if the document includes many photographs.

Care of photographs

- Paper clips should never be used on photographs.
- Pencil marks on the back of an unmounted photograph make an indentation.
- Mailing without protection is dangerous to prints. Merely marking of 'Do not fold' is not enough. Prints should be placed between two heavy pieces of cardboard.
- Face to face mailing or handling of prints from one department to another should be avoided. Dirt particles may get in between prints and damage not only one print but two at the same time.
- Finger prints can cause much damage to a print. Oil from the finger can stay on the print surface and if strong enough can show up on a halftone negative.

Graham W B. 1987. *Complete Guide to Pasteup*, 3rd edn, p. 71. Omaha, Nebraska, USA: Walter B Graham. 236 pp.

You have used an exact copy of an illustration from someone else's work.	Figure 4 A typical graphite block heat exchanger (reproduced from Hewitt 1990)
You have redrawn an illustration from someone else's work.	Figure 4.2 Apparatus for examining isoclinics in a stressed transparent model (redrawn from Alexander 1983)
You have adapted someone else's data on figure, and incorporated it into a table or figure of your own.	Figure 3.5 Schematic diagram of AFLP analysis (adapted from Vos et al. 1995)

Silyn-Roberts H. 2000. *Writing for Science and Engineering: papers, presentations and reports*, p. 174. Oxford, UK: Butterworth Heinemann. 281 pp.

Give credit where it is due when you reproduce illustrations, with or without changes. The same form of acknowledgements applies to tables as well.

Handling and care of photographs

Because photographs are more or less 'given' images, a style manual cannot have much to say on the topic.

Things to avoid in a photograph

- Avoid showing billboards, company logos, etc.
- Make sure that photographs do not show distorted images: readers expect photographs to show the truth.
- In medical photographs, individuals must not ordinarily be identifiable; if in doubt, obtain a written permission from the 'subjects'.
- Avoid pictures of people with their backs turned towards the camera.

Handling photographs for print production

- Handle photographs and slides carefully and always by their edges. A thumbprint may be invisible to the naked eye but a scanner will surely pick it up. Similarly, dents caused by paper clips, holes left by stapling pins, heavy markings made on the reverse, etc. can all ruin a photograph.
- Keep each photograph in a separate envelope and keep all these envelopes in a stiff-backed envelope. Always close the flaps and guard against any photograph accidentally falling out of its envelope.
- Maintain a log of every photograph that is to appear in a document. If the total number of photographs is known, number them 1/*, 2/*, and so on where the asterisk represents the total number of photographs.
- Label each photograph. It is best to use a mailing label to write the details and then stick it to the back of the photograph.
- Show which is the right way up whenever it is not totally clear from the subject of the photograph. Mark the label with an upward-pointing arrow and write 'Top' next to the arrow.
- Make sure that you get all the photographs back from the printer at the earliest. Warn the owner of the photographs

Address: www.blackwell-science.com/elecmed/digilla.htm

Resource

Books & CDs | Journals | Search | Home

Electronic artwork

Information for authors

Welcome to our online graphics resource for authors

◀ Technical Development
◀ Guidelines for Authors

PostScript from any application

Electronic artwork frequently asked questions

Everything you always wanted to know about digital imaging...

Glossary and file types

Submitting your own electronic artwork helps cut publication time and gives you more control over how we present your data. To help you get the best, we have a few simple standards.

Line art
Encapsulated PostScript (EPS) or
800 dpi TIFF (CMYK colour or greyscale)

Continuous tone
250–300 dpi TIFF(CMYK colour or greyscale)

Combination figures
Encapsulated PostScript (EPS) or
800 dpi TIFF(CMYK colour or greyscale)

You don't need professional, expensive illustration software to create print quality figures. Create PostScript from any application.

Ready to submit your work? goto checklist

© 2002 Blackwell Science Ltd.
Last update 4 June 2002

Illustrations in electronic form

that photographs receive rough handling in the press and that slides are usually taken out of their mounts.
- It is difficult to get an exact match between a 35-mm slide and its image as printed because slides are viewed in transmitted light whereas a printed image is viewed in reflected light, which dulls the colour somewhat.
- Always use originals: photographs that appear in printed sources rarely work well as originals because the image has already been broken into dots before printing; what you see on paper is actually a pattern of dots and not the original image.

Scanning for printing and for display on screen

The foregoing detailed handling instructions are more likely to appear dated or irrelevant now as scanning becomes increasingly common. Here are some tips for producing illustrations in electronic or soft-copy form. A useful introduction is 'Submitting artwork electronically', published on the web by Blackwell Science.

Decide early on whether the illustration is meant to be viewed on screen or printed on paper: the choice you make will govern the resolution and file format. In general, images displayed on a PC screen are less sharp than printed images because the resolution of the screen is only 96 pixels per inch (for Windows). A picture in a JPEG format, for instance, is adequate for screen but will reproduce poorly on paper.

Illustrations in electronic form for printing

- Scan line illustrations (charts, diagrams, text, etc. that have no shades of grey) at a high resolution (800 dpi) and save them as EPS (encapsulated PostScript) or TIFF files. Avoid BMP (bitmap) files.
- Scan tone illustrations (photographs, paintings, etc.) at a resolution of 250 dpi to 300 dpi and save them as TIFF files. For better rendering of colours, prefer the CMYK format to RGB format.

Chapter 7 Figures of speech

Where you place illustrations on the page can cue a reader where to look next or visually link different ideas through the use of different line weights, different styles, subject matter, glyphs, and colours. For ideas on ways to place illustrations with a smooth visual flow in mind, look through comic books or illustrated children's stories and see how the writers and artists worked together to lead you around the pages. While comic books and children's stories may seem unlikely resources for technical documentation, they are excellent examples of effective collaboration between writers and illustrators, and demonstrate how different skills combine to present the flow of information.

Sun Microsystems. 1996. *Read Me First! A style guide for the computer industry*, p. 17. Upper Saddle River, New Jersey, USA: Prentice Hall. 260 pp.

Quote

Example

Centre figures on the width of the text column and centre the caption on the figure.

Example

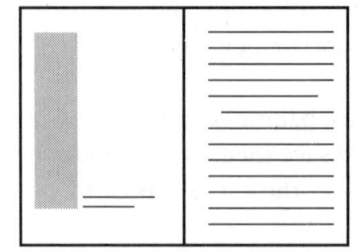

For narrow and tall figures, place the caption to the side of the figure. Place such figures near the outside margin (to the left on a left-hand page; to the right on a right-hand page).

Placing illustrations on a page

- Scan images that have both line and tone illustrations at a high resolution (800 dpi) and save them as EPS or TIFF files.
- Choose a size that corresponds to the final intended size and scan at that size; avoid resizing.

If illustrations are meant for screen only (on web pages or for documents in PDF format, for instance), save line illustrations as GIF (graphic interchange format) files and tone illustrations as JPEG files.

Integrating illustrations with text

In most documents, text fills more pages than pictures do but the pictures are usually noticed first, which is one reason to prepare them carefully. However, as users get down to reading a document, it is text that directs their flow. Therefore, it is important to ensure that every illustration is referred to in the text and to place the illustration as close to that point of reference as possible.

Many of the guidelines offered in the section on tables hold good for illustrations as well. The shape and size of a figure govern its placement. The following list offers some help in placing illustrations within the text pages.

- Place the figure immediately after the paragraph in which it is mentioned. If several figures are mentioned with a paragraph, they may be grouped.
- If a figure is less than the width of a page, centre it on page width. Centre the caption below the figure.
- Do not place any text to the right or left of the figure unless it is very small.
- If a figure is narrow but tall (like a tower), place the legend to its side instead of below. Place the figure to the right on a right-hand page and to the left on a left-hand page.
- If the figure takes up most of the space on a page, devote the entire page to that figure and its caption and leave the rest of the space blank. However, if there is enough space to fit at least 4 lines of text (or at least 10% of the number of lines

Ensure that a page with a large figure has at least 4 lines of text along with the figure and its caption. Place text at the top.

on a typical text page of that document), use that space for text. Place the text on top and then the figure, so that the body of the figure separates the text from the figure caption.

Bibliography

Bounford T. 2000
Digital Diagrams
London: Cassell. 192 pp.

Harris R L. 1997.
Information Graphics: a comprehensive illustrated reference
Atlanta, Georgia, USA: Management Graphics. 448 pp.

Tufte E R. 1997
Visual explanations: images and quantities, evidence and narrative
Cheshire, Connecticut, USA: Graphics Press. 158 pp.

Wainer H. 1997
Visual revelations: graphical tales of fate and deception from Napoleon Bonaparte to Ross Perot
New York: Copernicus (Springer-Verlag]. 180 pp.

Holmes N. 1993
The Best in Diagrammatic Graphics
Mies, Switzerland: Rotovision. 224 pp.

MacGregor A J. 1979
Graphics Simplified: how to plan and prepare effective charts, graphs, illustrations, and other visual aids
Toronto, Canada: University of Toronto Press. 64 pp.

Chapter 8 at a glance

Accurate identification of documents
What details to include, and why
Numbered references versus author–year system
Mentioning sources within text
- When shall I use 'et al.'?
- How shall I differentiate among two or more papers by the same author published in the same year?
- How shall I differentiate among two or more papers published in the same year by authors whose surnames are the same?
- How shall I cite a document that has no identifiable authors?
- How shall I cite an article from a well-known reference book?
- How shall I cite unpublished or yet-to-be-published documents?
- How shall I cite a document I have not examined (I am merely citing a reference taken from yet another document)?
- If two or more references are run together within parentheses, in what order shall I arrange them?
- How shall I punctuate text references?
- What about footnotes and endnotes?

Citing web pages and other electronic documents
Arranging and formatting references
- References? Bibliography? Further reading?
- Arranging the references alphabetically by author: some points of order
- Inverting the names of authors
- Shortening the given and middle names to initials
- Giving the names of journals in full
- Punctuation marks to separate different parts of a reference

Typographical formatting: using italics and boldface
Starting separate elements on new lines
References

8 ▶ Who said that?

citing and formatting sources of information

A technical document that makes no reference to any published source, acknowledges no one, and draws upon no earlier work is rare: nearly all reports, papers in journals, books, web pages, and other 'containers' in which technical information is packaged are but extensions of previous work. By providing detailed information about the sources that you consulted, you offer your readers the means to retrace your footsteps. Citing references is also a time-honoured method of giving credit where it is due—so much so that a veritable industry has been built up on citation-counts: how many times, and by whom and where, a paper has been cited.

Sources of information are *referred to* or *cited* in the text and *described* at the end of the text. Throughout this chapter, 'citation' means the mention of a source document within continuous text (or as the source of a table or a figure) and 'reference' means the complete description of the document at the end, usually as a part of a list titled 'References'.

This chapter answers some frequently asked questions including the following.

▹ How to cite a document that has no identifiable authors?
▹ What are the advantages of referring to documents by their author/s and the year of publication?
▹ When is it appropriate to use 'et al.' while listing the names of authors?
▹ Why is it advisable to spell out the titles of journals in full?
▹ How is a yet-to-be-published paper cited?

The chapter will also help you to master the technique of handling citations and references. You will learn not only to record the bibliographic details (author/s, year, title, publisher, page numbers, etc.) of a variety of documents, but also in what sequence to arrange the details, how to separate different items

Several studies of the accuracy of citations and presentations of others' assertions in the biomedical literature have revealed surprisingly high rates of error. An analysis of 300 randomly selected references in six frequently cited veterinary journals found major errors in 30% of them ··· Misquotation rates of 12% in medical journals ··· and 27% in surgical journals ··· have been reported.

Matthews J R, Bowen J M, and Matthews R W. 2000. *Successful Scientific Writing: a step-by-step guide for the biological and medical sciences*, 2nd edn, p. 15. Cambridge, UK: Cambridge University Press. 235 pp.

Address   www.shef.ac.uk/library/libdocs/ml-rs11.html

There is nothing more frustrating than coming to write up your dissertation only to find that you have forgotten to note publisher, page numbers, year, etc. for the publication you have referred to during your research.

As you embark on your review of the literature, keep a careful note of the full details of all the items you refer to. It is time-consuming but well worth it.

The University of Sheffield Library. 2000. Writing a bibliography

Whatever the style – and the variations from one publisher to the next are slight – the principle underlying all the forms is the same: it is implicit in the purpose of the reference footnote, which is to refer to you to sources. The note must be so framed that the reader can tell unfailingly the type of source cited—a manuscript or a printed article, a newspaper or a book, a letter or a conversation. These distinctions are important, for in estimating evidence sources are weighed not counted. Each kind of source impresses the reader in a different way. For example, a magazine article is generally written with more care than a newspaper column but probably with less than a book.

Barzun J and Graff H F. 1992. *The Modern Researcher*, p. 299. Boston, Massachusetts, USA: Houghton Mifflin. 409 pp.

of information with appropriate punctuation marks, and how to format a reference typographically (when to use bold, when to use italics, and so on).

Accurate identification of documents

It is perhaps natural to be annoyed by a copy editor's insistence on bibliographic details. The editor does realize that facts are far more important than the mechanics of presenting them; in fact, it is easy for a copy editor to put your references in the required format—what is difficult, if not impossible, is to supply missing details. The copy editor can take out a comma where it is not wanted or add one where it is necessary but can neither pinpoint the page number of the original document on which the table you have reproduced is printed nor divine who published the source document.

Remember, therefore, to record the necessary details for every document that you may be required to refer to in your paper. This is all the more important for documents that you may not get to examine again. Cross-check whatever you have recorded with the original at least once: it is far too common, for example, to write 1967 instead of 1976, Tewari instead of Tiwari, and Jones P R instead of Jones R P—a reference mis-recorded is a reference lost.

What are the necessary details? A simple enough question, but one that has no simple answer, because the details that you need to record depend on the kind of document it is: a paper in a journal, a web page, a book, an annual report of an organization, a paper in a volume of conference proceedings, a report, a thesis, a standard, a patent, a newspaper report, a software package, and so on. However, you will probably record the relevant details if you keep in mind that readers need these details to trace the document. A typical reference citation should

- identify the source precisely;
- describe it sufficiently; and
- guide the readers adequately if they wish to obtain the document.

Citations in text

Some information is already available on presenting tabular information. The recommendations cover three broad areas, namely editorial, ergonomic, and typographic; and examples of each are, respectively, **Finney (1986)**, **Ehrenberg (1981)**, and **Clark (1981)**. **Hartley (1994)** weaves all the strands together in a concise chapter on tables and graphs in his book *Designing Instructional Text*. A comprehensive review of literature is provided by Lefrere (1989) and a recent British Standard is BS 7581: 1992 *Guide to presentation of tables and graphs* **(BSI 1992)**.

Reference list

References

BSI. 1992. BS 7581: 1992. Guide to presentation of tables and graphs. London: British Standards Institution. 24 pp.

Clark N. 1981. Sample pages and specifications: Monthly Petroleum Statement. Los Altos, California: Dolby Associates. 20 pp.

Ehrenberg A S C. **1981.** The problem of numeracy. *The American Statistician* 35 (2): 67-71

Finney D J. **1986.** On presenting tables and diagrams. *Journal of Scholarly Publishing* 17: 327-342

Hartley J. **1994.** *Designing Instructional Text*. 3rd edn. London: Kogan Page. 183 pp.

What details to include, and why

A reference, no matter how you format it, should answer the usual questions, namely Who? When? What? Where? How much? and so on. A reference should also indicate the kind of document. Consider the following example: *Natural Resources Forum* **16**: 33. Here, you have all the information necessary to track the paper down—all you need to do is to pick volume 16 of *Natural Resources Forum* and open it on page 33. But is this description sufficient? By telling the readers (1) who wrote the paper (R K Pachauri, S Gupta, and M Mehra; (2) when it was published (1992); (3) what it is all about (A reappraisal of WRI's estimate of greenhouse gas emissions); and (4) how long it is (6 pages, the first *and the last* page numbers, or 'inclusive' page numbers, being 33 and 38), you help readers a great deal.

Is the paper recent? Are its authors known to me? What is the scope and main concern? How long is it? (How thoroughly or extensively has the topic been dealt with? How much will it cost to photocopy?)—a full reference answers all such questions.

Take another example: Dasgupta B, Sivaramakrishnan K C, and Buch M N. *Urbanization in India: basic services and people's participation*, Institute of Social Sciences, New Delhi. The bibliographic details tell you little about the document. No date is given, so you cannot know whether it is recent or dated; you cannot be certain whether it is an internal document, meant for the staff of the Institute of Social Sciences, or whether it has been formally published; you have no idea whether it is a substantial document – running to, say, 60 pages or more – or a brief memo.

If you are citing a paper presented at a conference, symposium, workshop, etc., you should tell the reader when and where the event was held and who organized it. If the proceedings have been published, mention the title of the proceedings volume, names of its editors and publishers, and the total number of pages as well.

> Many different styles of referencing have developed over the years, and indeed, there have been (different) national standards agreed in the USA (ANSI 1978), Europe (ISO 1987), and the UK (BSI 1989). However, few journals appear to follow these standards precisely, perhaps in view of the fact that each one of them allows a degree of choice. Today variation seems to run rife, and this is promulgated by computer-based systems for preparing references such as EndNote, Procite, and Reference Manager. Each of these systems allows authors to create more than 300 ways of presenting references. (The EndNote Manual provides illustrations of 17 different settings.)
>
> Hartley J. 2002. On choosing typographic settings for reference lists. *Social Studies of Science* **32**: 917–932

> Also essential are the publication data of the work, to help the researcher get to the original. There is a good deal of variation in this data field. Some publishers offer the city and date; some give the publisher as well. Some give publisher, city, date. ⋯ the more information the readers have, the more likely they will be to find the item in question. ⋯ Publishers' names can be given in full (W W Norton and Company) or can be given in short form (Norton). Either way is acceptable, as long as the short form does not leave the reader in doubt.
>
> Berger S E. 1991. *The Design of Bibliographies: observations, references and examples*, p. 34. London: Mansell. 198 pp.

Often, the proceedings are published as a book, the title of which is different from the title of the conference. For instance, proceedings of the international conference *Evaluating the benefits of recreational fishing*, which was held in Vancouver in June 1999, were published under the title *Recreational Fisheries: ecological, economic and social evaluation* by Blackwell Science, Oxford, in 2002. Supply full information in such cases, supplementing the reference with the dates, venue, organizers, and the title of the conference.

If citing a thesis, mention the university and the degree for which it was submitted along with the year and the total number of pages.

For newspaper articles, mention the place of publication, the date, and the page and column numbers.

Annexe A illustrates the sample formats for a variety of documents.

Numbered references versus author-year system

There is no universally accepted way of presenting references. No two publishers use an identical format and, despite many committees, task forces, workshops, standards, and so on, a uniform method is not a reality as yet. The topic of references almost always gets a whole session to itself whenever science editors organize their conferences. However, two major systems are common: Vancouver, in which the references are serially numbered in the order in which they appear in the text and Harvard, in which the references are identified by their author/s and the year of publication. In both systems, full bibliographic details for each of the cited document are supplied at the end, the references appearing either in the order in which they are cited in the text or arranged alphabetically by the first author's surname.

Each system has its advantages and disadvantages. For example, the numbered system saves space but does not tell the reader who the authors are or how recent is the work being cited. Patricia Wright (1985), in *Designing Usable Texts*, maintains

> Address www.library.qmul.ac.uk/bmed/ITskills.htm
>
> Vancouver however can be difficult to use if you don't have an effective information management system. For example if you have numbered your references and compiled your reference list, and then you edit out a paragraph which takes out three references, and therefore three numbers, this will throw your entire numerical system. To avoid this you should use the Harvard system in the text as you write your drafts, and then translate the references into numbers when you are sure your piece of work is complete. Be careful!
>
> Hayles J. 2002. Citing references: medicine and dentistry. [online, Word document]

> The numbered system
>
> In this system, each reference is numbered in order of appearance in each chapter. References are listed at the ends of chapters (or, by chapter, at the end of the book).
>
> There are some disadvantages to this system. ⋯ It is also difficult for the reader to find at a later date any particular reference in the list of references, as they will not normally be listed alphabetically. Numbers in the text are less immediately informative to the reader, as they are not accompanied by the writer's name.
>
> However, there are some advantages ⋯ for some literary works – scientific biographies, collections of lectures, etc. – the numbered systems works well, as the references do not impede the flow of the text. With this system the list of references can be expanded to include some comment and extra information as well. This can dispense with the need for footnotes or unnecessary detail in the text itself.
>
> Isaacs A, Daintith J, and Martin E (eds). 1991. *The Oxford Dictionary for Scientific Writers and Editors*, p. 385. Oxford, UK: Clarendon Press. 389 pp.

Adam, Bryson, Carey, ~~Doyle, Enderby~~ 2001
Adam, Bryson, Carey et al. 2001
✗   ✓   ✗   ✓
et. al.   et.al.   *et al.*   et al.

> If a source has four or more authors, shorten the citation to include only the first three, followed by et al. Note that 'et' does not take a full stop but 'al' does. Set the phrase in normal type; do not use italics.

that 'although saving space, this · · · system detracts from the usability of the text because readers can have no idea whether the quoted source is familiar or not unless they interrupt their reading to consult the reference list and decode the numbers.'

A few other shortcomings of numbering the references are that (1) it is tedious having to renumber the references if you add or take out references and (2) the system becomes unwieldy if, in addition to the references, you want to use endnotes, because the endnotes will also have to be identified using another sequence (superscript numbers for references and superscript letters for endnotes, for example).

Mentioning sources within text

Use the author–year system for all documents unless indicated otherwise (for instance, if you are writing a research paper for a journal and the journal follows the numbered-references system). After a phrase or a sentence for which you wish to cite a source, add the author and year in parentheses. Sometimes, the year alone goes within parentheses, if the statement is directly attributed to its author. A few common queries on how to use the author–year system are answered below.

When shall I use 'et al.'?

Mention all the authors up to a maximum of three. If a document is authored by four or more authors, mention the first three and add 'et al.' (for *et alii*, which means 'and others' in Latin[a])

As in every matter of style concerning references, authorities differ over the use of et al. *Scientific Style and Format*, compiled by the Council of Biology Editors (now the Council of Science Editors), recommends that 'et al.' be abandoned altogether and replaced with 'and others', in accordance with the council's general preference for English terms and abbreviations (CBE Style Manual Committee 1994). Then there is the

---

[a] To be precise, *et alii* is masculine, *et aliae* is feminine, and *et alia* is neuter.

| Address | http://tejas.serc.iisc.ernet.in/currsci/dec252002/1429.pdf | Quote |

But, the changing face of publishing in science is most clearly evident in some of biology's megaprojects. The announcement of the 'Initial Sequencing and Comparative Analysis of the Mouse Genome' carried a simple author byline—Mouse Genome Sequencing Consortium. Readers must turn to the end of a long article to find a list of over two hundred authors from 46 different laboratories. Curiously, the paper carries another footnote which identifies 16 authors as having contributed to 'project leadership' (*Nature*, 2002, 420, 520–562).

Balram P. 2002. The mores of publishing in science [editorial]. *Current Science* **83**: 1429–1430

| Address | www.ecs.soton.ac.uk/~lac/ht99.pdf | Quote |

However, author co-citation studies have been limited by the number of authors that one can map with multidimensional scaling facilities in the SPSS statistical package. For example, they had to limit the maximum number of authors within the capacity of the multidimensional scaling routines. In 1980s, the limit was 40 authors and in 1990s, this number is raised to 100 authors.

Chen C and Carr L. 1999. Trailblazing the literature of hypertext: author co-citation analysis (1989–1998). 8 pp. Proceedings of the 10th ACM Conference on Hypertext. Darmstadt, Germany, 21–25 February 1999

Bose 2002a, Dutta 1997, Bose 2002b

Differentiate two or more papers published by the same author or set of authors in one year by attaching letters to the year.

Example

Smith A B 2002, Smith C D 2002

Use initials to differentiate among namesakes if the year is also the same.

matter of italics: et al. or *et al.*? The *Oxford Dictionary for Writers and Editors* prefers the plain or roman style to italics (Ritter 2000). Cambridge University Press, on the other hand, prefers italics (Butcher 1992).

The choice of Latin or English and roman or italics is a trivial matter of style: the cut-off point in the number of author before using 'and others' is not so trivial because on it depends whether a given author's name will appear in the citation at all. A common enough convention is that no matter what the cut-off point is for the use of 'and others' in text, all the authors are to be listed in the references section. However, as the average number of authors for a research paper continues to increase steadily, *Index Medicus*, published by the (u s) National Library of Medicine, has introduced an upper limit on the number of authors to be listed in the references section: it names all authors up to 25; if the number of authors exceeds 25, only the first 24 and the last author are named.

> How shall I differentiate among two or more papers by the same author published in the same year?

Label the references that have the same author–year combination by adding letters, assigning 'a' to the reference that occurs first, 'b' to the next, and so on.

> How shall I differentiate among two or more papers published in the same year by authors whose surnames are the same?

Identify namesakes by supplying their initials as well.

> How shall I cite a document that has no identifiable authors?

Annual reports of organizations, reports of committees, and standards are examples of documents that lack named authors. In such cases, the entity responsible for the document is taken as its author. The idea is to tell readers who the 'authority' is, so that they may judge for themselves how authentic the source is, whether it is a familiar one, and so on.

Chapter **8** Who said that?

When citing chapters or the Technical Summary from this report, please use the authors in the order given on the chapter frontpage, for example, Chapter 2 is referenced as:

Folland, C.K., T.R. Karl, J.R. Christy, R.A. Clarke, G.V. Gruza, J. Jouzel, M.E. Mann, J. Oerlemans, M.J. Salinger and S.-W. Wang, 2001: Observed Climate Variability and Change. In: *Climate Change 2001: The Scientific Basis*. Contribution of Working Group I to the Third Assessment Report of the Intergovernmental Panel on Climate Change [Houghton, J.T., Y. Ding, D.J. Griggs, M. Noguer, P.J. van der Linden, X. Dia, K. Maskell, and C.A. Johnson (eds.)]. Cambridge University Press, Cambridge, United Kingdom and New York, NY, USA, 881 pp.

Reference to the whole report is:

IPCC, 2001: *Climate Change 2001: The Scientific Basis*. Contribution of Working Group I to the Third Assessment Report of the Intergovernmental Panel on Climate Change [Houghton, J.T., Y. ding, D.J. Griggs, M. Noguer, P.J. van der Linden, X. Dai, K. Maskell, and C.A. Johnson (eds.)]. Cambridge University Press, Cambridge, United Kingdom and New York, NY, USA, 881 pp.

The Intergovernmental Panel on Climate Change offers explicit guidance on citing its technical reports.

Quote

Citation in text

In some parts of India, the fruits (capsules) of chilli are smeared with the oil of 'mahua' (*Madhuca longifolia*) to impart a shine (*Wealth of India* 1992).

Reference

Wealth of India. 1992. Capsicum. In *The Wealth of India: raw materials*, vol. 3: Ca-ci (revised edition), pp. 218-264. New Delhi: Council of Scientific and Industrial Research. 1877 pp.

Cite established reference sources by their titles and the year of publication.

Example

Names of organizations are usually abbreviated. If you think that readers may not be familiar with the abbreviation, rephrase the sentence so as to bring in the full name of the organization: 'Central Pollution Control Board has prescribed the maximum permissible levels for concentrations of some common air pollutants (CPCB 1986).' In listing the references alphabetically, it is the abbreviated version that decides the correct place in the sequence of that reference.

Choosing an appropriate 'author' is a matter of judgement. At times, the entity responsible for the document offers some guidance.

Editorials in some journals are usually unsigned. Use the title of the journal as the author, followed by the word 'editorial' within square brackets. In the list of references, treat the journal as the author.

How shall I cite an article from a well-known reference book?

Established reference sources, both general (*Encyclopaedia Britannica* and the *Oxford English Dictionary*) and specialized (the *Wealth of India* series, *Statistical Outline of India*, and *Census of India* reports), are best cited by their titles followed by the year of publication.

How shall I cite unpublished or yet-to-be-published documents?

Personal correspondence and discussions, internal memos and reports, and manuscripts are some examples of unpublished documents. Mention them in the text by their author and, instead of the year, add 'personal communication' or 'unpublished observations' as appropriate. Such citations do not figure at all in the list of references at the end. A paper submitted to a journal falls in the same category, namely unpublished observations, unless it has been accepted for publication.

> Make sure you read every reference yourself. This is an area where you do need to invest time. As the author, you are responsible for ensuring that the references you cite are accurate, and this means reading them in the original as well as tracking them back to their first appearance. Be obsessive about this. It is unlikely that anyone important will check them, but there is an important matter of principle: how much value can we put on a system that prizes itself on its integrity when a major part is full of inaccuracies?
>
> Albert T. 2000. *The A-Z of Medical Writing*, p. 111. London: BMJ Books. 145 pp.

✗ Some information is already available on presenting tabular information. The recommendations cover three broad areas, namely editorial, ergonomic, and typographic (Dawkins 2000, Cochrane 2001, Bryson 2002, and Adam 2003).

✓ Some information is already available on presenting tabular information. The recommendations cover three broad areas, namely editorial, ergonomic, and typographic (Adam 2003, Bryson 2002, Cochrane 2001, and Dawkins 2000).

When many citations appear together, arrange them alphabetically by authors—not chronologically).

✗ Wright, 1987   ✓ Wright 1987

✓ ✓ ✓
Sinnot, Dunn, and Dobzhansky 1958; Wright, Hull, and Black 1990; Wright, Lickorish, Hull et al. 1988

Skip the comma between author/s and year; insert a comma to separate authors within a single reference; insert a semicolon to separate one citation from the next.

To cite a paper that has been accepted for publication, supply the author's name and add 'in press' in place of the year. Put a comma after the author's name: Bose, in press. Supply the name and initials of the author, title of the paper, and title of the journal in the list of references.

How shall I cite a document I have not examined (I am merely citing a reference taken from yet another document)?

A short answer: Don't. Reproducing information without cross-checking it against the original source can be embarrassing if the information turns out to be incorrect. However, if you must cite a source at secondhand, make it clear to the reader that you are doing so by giving both the original source (which you have not seen) and the secondary source (which you have).

If two or more references are run together within parentheses, in what order shall I arrange them?

If two or more references are run together in parentheses, arrange them in alphabetical order by the author. Some publishers prefer to list such references in chronological order.

How shall I punctuate text references?

Use minimal punctuation. Insert just one character-space, not a comma, between the author and the year: Bowman 2003. Use a comma to separate one author from the other: Ghosh, Mittal, and Puri 1994. Use a semicolon between references if two or more references are run together within parentheses: (Sinclair, Vadez, and Chenu 2003; Sirohi, Vijaipal and Khanna 2000; Sridhar and Rant 2002).

What about footnotes and endnotes?

Citations in text supply information about documentary sources but technical documents often require such additional devices as footnotes and endnotes to present relevant supplementary information. Both footnotes and endnotes contain

Chapter **8** Who said that?

| Address | www.press.uchicago.edu/Misc/Chicago/721833.html | Quote |

A monstrous variation on the parenthesis is the content footnote. What, after all, is a content footnote but material that one is either too lazy to integrate into the text or too reverent to discard? Reading a piece of prose that constantly dissolves into extended footnotes is profoundly disheartening.

> Robinson P. 2002. The philosophy of punctuation in *Opera, Sex, and Other Vital Matters*. Chicago, Illinois, USA: University of Chicago Press. 350 pp.

| Address | http://deseretnews.com/dn/view/0,1249,455031878,00.html | Quote |

Here's the flip side of the digital age's magic act: it's also making information disappear. 'The digital history of this nation is imperiled by the very technology that is used to create it,' said Librarian of Congress James Billington. In fact, according to data from the Library of Congress, the average Web page has a lifespan of just a couple of months. Of all the Web content made in 1998, nearly half had disappeared by 1999. 'Much of what has been created is no longer accessible,' Billington said. 'And much of what disappears is important, one-of-a-kind material that can never be recovered, but will be desperately looked for.'

> *The Washington Post*. 2003. Library aims to save digital data. [News item dated 15 February 2003]

supplementary information that, if woven into the text, could obstruct its flow. The difference lies in the kind of information and how much of it is supplied. The current practice is to keep footnotes very brief (no more than a few words) and to use them to supply such incidental information as changes in names of countries or administrative entities, conversion factors ($1 = Rs 30, or whatever), and explanations of non-English terms.

Endnotes are more extensive and offer elaborations, lengthy explanations, alternative views, derivations of formulae, and so on.

In text, flag footnotes with letters of the alphabet (set as superscripts and in italics) and endnotes with superscript numerals. Footnotes, by definition, are explained at the foot of the page whereas endnotes are placed at the end of the text but before references (so that citations, if any, used in the endnotes can be included in the list of references).

Citing web pages and other electronic documents

As access to the Internet increases, researchers rely more and more on such electronic documents, as web pages and files in PDF (portable document format). However, so long as the purpose in referring to other sources remains the same, considerations that govern the format for citing printed documents apply equally to electronic documents. In fact, it is even more important to cite such sources accurately because they are more likely to be accessible to your readers.

Essentially, adopt the same format and sequence as that explained in detail later for printed documents: author, date, title of the document, and its precise location. Enclose the 'web address', or URL (uniform resource locator) to use the technical term, in angled brackets, e.g. <www.teriin.org> and supply the date on which you last accessed the document.

You may choose to provide the URL, along with other relevant information, only at the point of mention and confine the reference section only to details of printed documents. The

Chapter **8** Who said that?

Atkins P. 1995

Atkins P. 1998

Atkins P and Bland S. 1992

Atkins P and Carey A J. 1990

Atkins P, Doyle A J, and Black D. 1990

Atkins P, Doyle A J, and Carey A J. 1987

Atkins P, Carey A J, Bland S, Felker K. 1992

Atkins P, Bland S, Doyle A J, Gold K. 1998

Atkins P, Appleby G A, Hindon K, Lamb D. 2000

Example

Up to three authors, arrange the list alphabetically; with four or more authors, follow chronological order.

advantage is that the URLs can be easily turned into links as and when the document is published on the web. Walker and Taylor (1998) comprehensively cover the topic of citing electronic sources.

Arranging and formatting references

References? Bibliography? Further reading?

The usual heading for the list of documents, with full bibliographic details of each, is 'References' because the documents have been *referred to* in the text.

Use the heading 'Bibliography' for the list of sources that you have consulted while preparing your paper/report. However, particular statements within the text of the document are not linked to specific lines within these sources.

Use 'Further reading' as a heading for a list of published documents that you recommend to readers for obtaining additional information.

Arranging the references alphabetically by author: some points of order

Alphabetic order is straightforward but arranging several papers by the same author, either singly or with others, may pose problems. If the same author has published some papers singly and others jointly, single-author publications come first, followed by those with only two authors and then by those with three authors. In a list of papers in which Atkins is the first author, for example, all the documents in which Atkins is the sole author come first, in chronological order. These are followed by papers written jointly by Atkins with *one* other collaborating author. These are arranged alphabetically by the name of the second author, Atkins and Bland coming before Atkins and Carey. These are in turn followed by papers written by Atkins jointly with *two* other authors. At the end of the list are papers that have more than three authors, and these are listed in chronological order; the names of collaborating authors are not taken into account in deciding on the order

      ✗   ✗
Wright P, A J Hull, and D K Black
          ✓   ✓
Wright P, Hull A J, and Black D K
   ✗   ✗   ✗
Wright, P, Hull, A J, and Black, D K

Invert the names of *all* authors, not just that of the first author, so all authors appear with their surnames first. Skip the comma between a surname and initials.

        ✗   ✗
Watson, James and Crick, Frances H C
       ✓   ✓
Watson J and Crick F H C
       ✗   ✗
Watson J. and Crick F. H. C.
       ✓   ✓
Watson J and Crick F H C

Shorten given and middle names to initials. Separate initials with space, not a full stop.

✗ Proc. Nat. Acad. Sci. USA
    Ind. J. Agric. Sci.
    Curr. Sci.

✓ Proceedings of the National Academy of Sciences, USA
    Indian Journal of Agricultural Sciences
    Current Science

Spell out journal titles in full.

because, in text, only the first three authors are named, followed by 'et al.'.

Inverting the names of authors

In reference lists, names of authors are inverted, i.e. the family name or surname comes before the initials. Invert the names of all authors, not just of the first author. The names are inverted because, in alphabetizing the list, references are sorted by surnames.

In Chinese names, it is normal to place family names (surnames) before given names. In reference lists, such names are therefore printed without inverting them. Correct handling of names of authors is a topic by itself and beyond the scope of this handbook; IFLA (1996) is a standard reference on the topic.

Shortening the given and middle names to initials

Not only are the names inverted but they are also shortened by replacing first and middle names with initials. Note that initials are not followed by full stops but only with single spaces.

Giving the names of journals in full

Always spell out journal titles in full. This practice identifies the source unambiguously. For example, 'Trop. Agric.' could be either *Tropical Agriculturist* (published from Colombo) or *Tropical Agriculture* (published from Trinidad).

Spelling out journal titles in full also solves the problem of how to abbreviate the titles. Again, there is no universally agreed system for shortening journal titles. Note that titles of journals and books are set in headline style (Capitalizing Each Significant Word).

Punctuation marks to separate different parts of a reference

Full stop Full stop is the most frequent mark. Use it to separate the author from the year; the year from the title of the

```
        ✗           ✗                      ✗         ✗
Annals of applied biology          The origin of species
        ✓           ✓                      ✓         ✓
Annals of Applied Biology          The Origin of Species
```

> Capitalize the first and every significant word in titles of journals and books. Articles, joining conjunctions ('and', 'but', 'or', etc.), and prepositions are seldom capitalized.

```
Watson J D and Crick F H C. 1953. Molecular structure of
nucleic acids: a structure for deoxyribose nucleic
acid. Nature 171: 737-738
```

> Full stops separate names of authors and the year of publication, the year of publication and the title of the paper, and the title of the paper and the title of the journal.

```
Micklos D A, Freyer G A, and Crotty D. 2003. DNA
Science: a first course, 2nd edn. Cold Spring Harbor,
New York: Cold Spring Harbor Laboratory Press. 575 pp.
```

> Commas separate one author from another. A colon separates the title of a book from its subtitle, and the place of publication from the name of the publisher.

```
Ramachandran V S and Hubbard E M. 2003. Hearing colors,
tasting shapes. Scientific American 288 (5): 53-59
```

> Brackets enclose the issue numbers of magazines, which paginate each issue separately. Journals, on the other hand, continue the pagination across issues within a volume.

```
Barnes M R and Southan C. 2003. Internet resources for
the geneticist, pp. 21–37 in Bioinformatics for
Geneticists, edited by M R Barnes and Ian C Gray.
Chichester, UK: Wiley. 408 pp.
```

> An en dash, not a hyphen, shows the range of pages.

```
Pitcher T J and Hollingworth C E (eds). 2002.
Recreational Fisheries: ecological, economic and
social evaluation. Oxford, UK: Blackwell Science. 271
pp. [Fish and Aquatic Resources Series 8, series editor
Tony J Pitcher]
```

> Square brackets enclose supplementary information.

article; and the title of the article from the title of the source (a journal, conference proceedings, multi-authored book, etc.) when references are set out 'run on'. The style used in this handbook employs fewer full stops because some parts of a reference always begin on a fresh line.

Commas Use commas to separate one author from another and the title of a newspaper from its date.

Colons Use a colon between the place of publication and the publisher, and between the volume number of a journal and the page numbers. Note that a colon never has a space before but always has a space after.

Parentheses Enclose the issue number in parentheses and place the parentheses after the volume number but before the colon. Most *journals* begin the first issue of a volume with page 1 and continue numbering the pages serially irrespective of the issue number: for instance, if the first issue runs to 128 pages, the next issue starts from page 129 and so on until the volume is complete. However, most *magazines* begin each issue with a fresh numbering sequence: each issue begins with page 1. The issue number is therefore essential for complete identification of magazine articles.

En dash Always use an en dash between page numbers. The Windows code for an en dash is Alt + 0150. An en dash (–) is twice as long as a hyphen (-).

Square brackets Enclose additional information in square brackets. For instance, in documents in which each paragraph is numbered, supply the page numbers as well as the paragraph number, using square brackets around the paragraph number. If the reference is to a data-book, supply not only the page number on which the table appears but also mention its number and title, enclosing that information in square brackets. Details of conferences, serial numbers or other identification codes for reports, and series numbers are all examples of those items of information that are enclosed in square brackets.

Full stops, colons, commas, parentheses, en dashes, and square brackets are about the only marks you will need to punctuate a bibliographic reference.

Chapter **8** Who said that?

Barnes M R and Southan C. 2003
Internet resources for the geneticist, pp. 21-37 in
Bioinformatics for Geneticists, edited by M R Barnes and
Ian C Gray. Chichester, UK: Wiley. 408 pp.

Example

Setting the smaller element (title of an article or a paper, of a chapter within a book, and so on) in boldface makes it stand out in a bibliography or a list of references, a practice followed in this handbook.

Design and layout of references

Typographical formatting: using italics and boldface

References usually identify a smaller unit within a larger unit: a paper (the smaller element) within a journal (the larger element), a paper within a proceedings volume, a chapter within a book, and so on. Set the larger element (the source document) in italics. If the reference mentions only one element (a single book or a whole special issue of a journal, for example), then that is set in italics.

Setting the titles in bold italics makes them stand out in a bibliography or a list of references, a practice followed in this handbook. The only other item to be set in boldface is the volume number of a journal.

Starting separate elements on new lines

If space is not a constraint, break up the entire reference into several lines. Author/s and year appear in one line, the title of the article appears on the next line, and the location (title of the journal, volume number and page numbers for journal articles; place of publication, publisher, and the total number of pages for a book) is given on yet another line. If the information meant to appear in one line spills over to the next line, the second line is indented one space.

References

Butcher J. 1992.
***Copy-Editing**: the Cambridge handbook for editors, authors and publishers*, 3rd edn, p. 253.
Cambridge, UK: Cambridge University Press. 471 pp.

CBE Style Manual Committee. 1994.
***Scientific Style and Format**: the CBE manual for authors, editors, and publishers*, 6th edn, p. 191.
Chicago, Illinois, USA: Council of Biology Editors. 825 pp.

International Federation of Library Associations. 1996.
***Names of Persons**: national usages for entry in catalogues*. 4th edn.
Munich, Germany: K G Saur. 263 pp.

Chapter **8** Who said that?

> Quote
>
> The aim of a citation in the List of References is to allow the information to be retrieved again. You therefore need to provide the information that will allow your reader to retrieve the material you cite.
>
> There are minor variations in the way the lists are formatted for different house styles. It is essential to establish the formatting required, and to keep to it rigidly and consistently.
>
> There are standard abbreviations for the journals. Don't make them up—refer to one of the standard publications found in libraries. One of the most convenient is Periodical Title Abbreviations (1996), 10th edition, volumes 1–3, edited by L G Alkire, and published by Gale Research Company, Detroit, Michigan. Volume 1 enables you to search by abbreviation, Volume 2 by title.
>
> Be sure that every full stop or comma is in the right place, and all other aspects of the formatting are correct. Formatting of references is riddled with convention, and assessors often check this area very thoroughly.
>
> Silyn-Roberts H. 2000. *Writing for Science and Engineering: papers, presentations and reports*, pp. 175–176. Oxford, U K: Butterworth Heinemann. 281 pp.

Ritter R M (ed.). 2000.
The Oxford Dictionary for Writers and Editors, 2nd edn, p. 108.
Oxford, UK: Oxford University Press. 404 pp.

Walker J R and Taylor T. 1998.
The Columbia Guide to Online Style
New York: Columbia University Press. 218 pp.

Wright P. 1985.
Editing: policies and processes, pp. 63–96
in *Designing Usable Texts*, edited by T M Duffy and R Waller.
New York: Academic Press. 423 pp.

Chapter 9 at a glance

Strategy for effective communication
Effective opening
Effective closing
Format and style for letters
Format and style for fax messages
Format and style for e-mails
   Tips for effective e-mails
Bibliography

9 ▶ Remote control

effective letters, faxes, and e-mails

Not everybody writes research papers and project reports but all write letters, fax messages, e-mail messages, or memos—the most common forms of writing at the workplace. Conventions of form and style make these communications more efficient. This chapter sets out the common conventions, offers advice on crafting messages to make them effective, and includes tips on how to customize messages to suit each channel of communication: what font works best for fax messages, how to highlight parts of e-mail messages, and so on. Here are some questions the chapter attempts to answer.

▶ Where should you place the subject line in a business letter, before the salutation or after the salutation?
▶ Which is the more appropriate ending for a business letter, 'Yours faithfully' or 'Yours sincerely'?
▶ Why is it advisable to keep photocopies of pages received through a fax machine?
▶ What alternatives to bold or italics are available in e-mail messages?

Strategy for effective communication

The first thing to remember is that you have competition: whomsoever you are writing to is not likely to be simply waiting for your letter to arrive, and even when it does arrive, it is not likely to arrive by itself. Other tasks may also be claiming your correspondent's attention: a meeting to attend; a letter to dictate; a visitor or a deadline to meet; or a troublesome laboratory experiment. If your letter looks as though it is a lot to read, it is more likely to be set aside: if it looks easy to read and, even more important, begins in a way that holds the reader's interest, you have won half the battle—hence the advice to begin the letter with something that would interest your reader; to always assign a subject to every letter; and to use a clear, easy-to-read font and adequate line-spacing.

| Address | www.writingandeditingatwork.com/writingtips.html | Quote |

Encourage readers to turn to the second page of a sales-generating letter by ending the first page in the middle of a sentence.
Smith L A. 2003. 18 Tips for writing business letters

| Address | www.lgu.ac.uk/langstud/je103/letters.htm | Quote |

Closing paragraph
- Expected outcome
- Request for action
- Details of deadlines
- Polite, reassuring close

Excerpt from a web page on business communication published by the London Guildhall University

Many people have speculated over the last 80 years or so about the possibilities of using colored paper to boost response-rates to surveys and questionnaires, and several studies have been carried out. ··· In this investigation we pooled together the results from all the experimental studies known to us on the topic and we carried out a meta-analysis to see if there might be a positive effect for colored paper overall. ··· we found no significant differences between the response rates to white and to colored paper in general. However, when we considered separately the most common colors used, it appeared that pink paper had the greatest effect.

Hartley J and Rutherford A. 2003. The effects of using colored paper to boost response-rates to surveys and questionnaires. *Journal of Technical Writing and Communication* **33**: 29–40

Effective opening

Remember also that the first few lines of a letter stand the greatest chance of being read and have the most impact. Therefore, it pays to spend some time crafting an effective opening. The subject line – place it immediately below the salutation and in bold – and the opening line together should tell readers what your letter is all about and, more important, how it is of some concern to them. If nothing else, it should pull the reader into the body of the letter. 'So what?' or 'Where do I come in?' by way of a response is the surest indicator of a poor opening.

Effective closing

Effective letters never leave their recipients in doubt as to what the sender of the letter expects to happen next. End letters by requesting their recipients to do whatever it is that you would like them to do and, where applicable, also tell them what your next step is going to be. For instance, if you have asked for information, remind the reader and say how to send it to you. If you have asked for an appointment, say that you would get in touch with them or their office as a follow-up. Never leave your readers wondering what they should do next.

Always make it a point to work into your letter some deadline. Set a date by which you expect a response even when the exact date is of little consequence to you. Where appropriate, offer good reasons for the deadline. Mentioning a deadline serves two purposes: firstly, it makes it more likely that the recipient will respond to it than when the request is totally open-ended; secondly, it serves to set a date for the reminder (and provides a good opening for it).

Format and style for letters

Some points of style are explained below. It is assumed that you are using a printed letterhead to type the letter. However, the recommendations are not specific to any particular letterhead.

| Address | www.faculty.sfasu.edu/sjennings/ 2002%20ABC%20Johnson-Jennings.ppt |

Quote

When you receive a business letter, what importance do you place on its appearance and format?

Very important; question credibility of message/sender if document contains formatting errors: 40%

Important; creates a positive (or negative) impression on sender: 60%

Johnson B and Jennings S E. 2002. Business correspondence formats: what is important? Paper presented at the 67th Annual Convention of the Association for Business Communication, 23–26 Oct., Cincinnati, Ohio

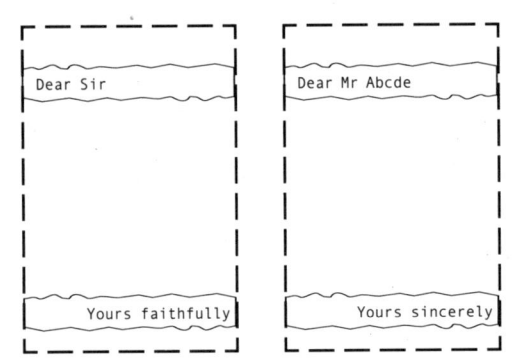

Example

Dear Sir … Yours faithfully

Dear Mr Abcde … Yours sincerely

If the letter is addressed by name, choose 'Yours sincerely' as the complimentary close.

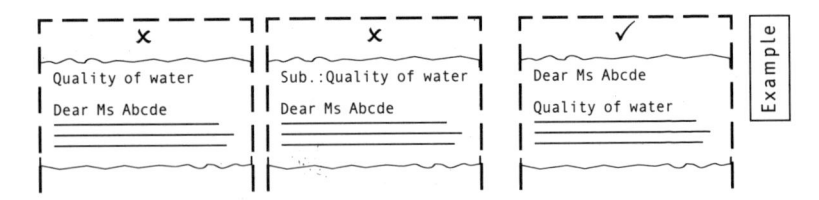

Example

✗ Quality of water / Dear Ms Abcde

✗ Sub.:Quality of water / Dear Ms Abcde

✓ Dear Ms Abcde / Quality of water

Place the subject-line *after* the salutation. Make it bold. Do not use such tags as 'Subject' or 'sub.'.

Letters: format and style

- Place the date at top right. The format for the date is date-month-year, as in 21 June 2003, with the month spelt out in full. The month is not followed by a comma. Use all the four digits for the year.
- Do not use a 'leading zero' in single-digit dates, that is, type these without inserting a zero to before the single digit; for instance, type 9 May and not 09 May.
- Allow up to 6 lines for the inside address; edit longer addresses if necessary and make up for shorter addresses by inserting as many blank lines as necessary to make the address block 6 lines long.
- For all Indian addresses, the last line should invariably be the delivery post office and the PIN code, separated with a spaced en dash. Do not include the state or the district in a postal address so long as you are using the correct PIN code. For addresses outside India, the last line consists of the name of the country. See Annexe D for more information.
- The salutation could be by name or simply Dear Sir/Madam, Dear Subscriber, Dear Manager, or whatever. Omit the comma after the salutation—it serves no purpose.
- Set the subject line in bold. Do not use a tag such as Subject: or Sub. as a part of the subject line; its position and appearance make it obvious that it is the subject.
- Put the complimentary close to the right, aligned vertically with the date. Use 'Yours sincerely' if the letter is addressed to an individual by name – the salutation would reflect this – and 'Yours faithfully' if the salutation is not by name. This distinction is seldom followed in the US.
- Type the sender's name below the space left for the signature, aligned vertically with the 'Y' of 'Yours'. Do not put brackets around the name.
- On the same line, indicate enclosure/s, if any, by typing 'ENC' or 'ENCS' (for more than one) to the left. Also indicate the numbers of separate enclosures, as in ENCS 4.
- You may indicate what the enclosures are if you wish, and if space permits. Type them as a numbered list, giving a separate line to each item.

Chapter **9** Remote control

```
ENCS 3    Yours sincerely          ENC       Yours sincerely
                                   CC ____, ____, ____
```
Example

Indicate enclosures, if any, by ENC (if only one) or ENCS (if more than one). If copies of the letter are to be circulated, indicate that with 'cc' followed by the list of those to whom copies are to be sent.

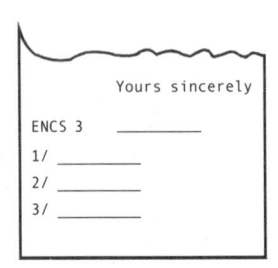

```
          Yours sincerely
ENCS 3    _____
1/ _____
2/ _____
3/ _____
```
Example

If space permits, list each enclosure.

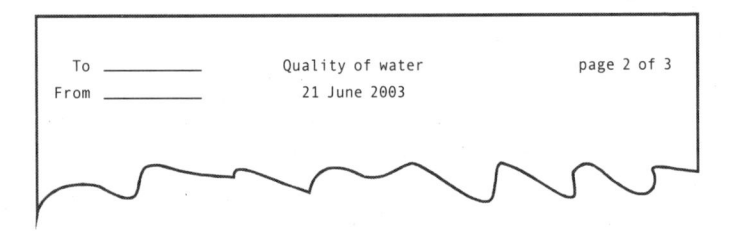

```
To   _____    Quality of water       page 2 of 3
From _____    21 June 2003
```
Example

Use a page header on continuation sheets

Faxing breaks type into coarse digital elements, a process as unpredictable as photocopying, but almost always worse. Letters can become black blobs or even appear to transform into other letters due to the insensitivity of the process.

Quote

    Burke C. 1993. *Designing Business Documents*, p. 36. Redhill, Surrey, UK: Monotype Typography. 36 pp. [Monotype Desktop Solutions series]

Fax messages: format and style

- The last item in a typical business letter is an indication of its distribution — the 'cc' tag (a leftover of the days when carbon copies were common). This forms the last line and a list of those who are to receive copies of the letter immediately follows, with one space in between (not a colon). The symbol 'bcc', for blind carbon copy, is sometimes used on *copies* – and not on the original – to indicate that the recipient of the letter does not know that copies are being sent to others (whose names follow the tag 'bcc').
- For letters that continue beyond a page, use blank sheets of the same size as the printed letterhead as 'continuation sheets'. Use a page header on these pages to display some identifying information: the sender's name, the recipient's name, subject and date, and page number should be ample in most cases.

Format and style for fax messages

- Use a font that can compensate for the inevitable degradation of the image (Verdana set in 9 points works very well) because fax messages are printed out on low-resolution printers.
- For added readability, introduce extra spacing (0.1 or 0.2 point) between letters to compensate for the low-resolution printing, which often thickens individual characters and makes them appear to be touching each other.
- Display prominently the number to which the fax is to be sent (destination), which makes it easier for those who handle outgoing faxes.
- Display the recipient's name and department, if any, which makes it easier for those responsible for distributing the incoming faxes.
- Display the total number of pages in the message to help in collating the message at the receiving end (since the pages are printed out individually).
- Avoid sheets longer than A4. Also, leave the bottom 3 cm blank for fax messages sent to USA and Canada because the

Chapter **9** Remote control

> Address: http://office.microsoft.com/Assistance/9798/newfilters.aspx
>
> The Junk and Adult Content filters work by looking for key words. This file is a description of exactly which words the filter looks for and where the filter looks for them.
> First 8 characters of From are digits
> ˙Subject contains 'advertisement'
> Body contains 'money back'
> Body contains 'cards accepted'
> Body contains 'removal instructions'
> Body contains 'extra income'
> Subject contains '!' AND Subject contains '$'
> Subject contains '!' AND Subject contains 'free'
> ...
>
>> Avoid using characters, words, or phrases commonly used in spam or junk mails.

> Above all, remember that e-mail is *not* conversation. Anything you put down is recorded, and as such, can be sent elsewhere, printed out, and extracted from the hard drive of your computer or that of your recipients, at a later date (erasing a message doesn't make it disappear). In short, e-mail is potentially public. Again, think before you write and send.
> Montgomery S L. 2002. *The Chicago Guide to Communicating Science*, p. 191. Chicago, Illinois, U S A: University of Chicago Press. 228 pp. [Chicago Guides to Writing, Editing, and Publishing]

standard paper in these countries is slightly shorter (11 inches, whereas an A4 sheet is 11.7 inches).
- Keep the fax message to a single page, as far as possible. If necessary, keep the additional sheets as annexes or attachments, so that the first page forms a complete communication in itself, including the sender's name and the signature following a complimentary close.
- Keep photocopies of fax messages that you receive; the originals tend to fade quickly.

Format and style for e-mails

For sheer convenience, speed, and economy, e-mail cannot be bettered. Again, it is this ease that is both an asset and a liability: asset because it can move large volumes of text easily and fast: liability because it is free of the checks that the slower modes impose automatically. A few technical constraints also apply, such as the body of an e-mail message being restricted to the 128 ASCII characters. The sheer quantity of e-mails – it is so easy to forward them to others – also means that people have less time to spend on any one e-mail message.

Tips for effective e-mails

- Always use the subject field; do not leave it blank. Avoid using characters, words, or phrases commonly used in spam or junk mails.
- Keep e-mail messages short; one screenful is ideal. Send more detailed information only when requested.
- Include your e-mail address in the body of the message. Also, make a signature file with your name, postal address, fax, etc. and append the file to all messages that you send.
- Use a large point size and wide margins if you are composing the message in a word processor and intend to paste it into the message field later. This ensures that the lines in your message appear intact instead of being displayed at the receiver's end as a series of very short lines alternating with lines of normal length.

Be considerate when sending attachments. Consider the size of the attachment. Files smaller than 100 kilobytes are generally acceptable. You may want to warn your correspondent with a separate e-mail message if you are sending any attachment that is longer. A 2-megabyte high-resolution graphic, for example, could take a long time to download and could cause the recipient's Internet mailbox to overflow, preventing further e-mail from being delivered.

Jones D and Lane K. 2002. *Technical Communication: strategies for college and the workplace*, p. 503. New York: Longman. 782 pp.

| Address | www.wilbers.com/Email.htm |

By its nature e-mail communication encourages a personal, informal style of writing, a feature most people view as attractive. Writers get into trouble, however, when they assume that readers can actually hear the inflection of their voices. Although e-mail may be more like oral communication than traditional forms of written communication, it's still writing, not speaking.

To guard against this type of misunderstanding, take this simple precaution: Include a goodwill statement in every message you send.

Rather than 'Fine', write 'Fine. Happy to do it.' Rather than write 'Please come prepared to discuss the report,' add another sentence: 'As always, I value your experience and insight.'

Wilbers S. 1999. Be careful of the drawbacks in hasty use of e-mail. [First published in the *Minneapolis Star Tribune*, 3 September 1999.]

Graphic devices in e-mails

- After you have exchanged a couple of mails, you can dispense with the salutation and the complimentary close—messages sent by e-mail are regarded as sufficiently informal to dispense with this formality.
- Confine yourself to ASCII characters: do not use subscripts or superscripts, italics, bold, bullets, etc. in e-mail messages. You could use the hash mark (#) for bullets instead. To indicate *bold* letters, enclose them within asterisks; indicate _italics_ by using an underscore on either side of the matter.
- Use the 3-letter currency code instead of symbols: GBP for £, JPY for ¥, etc. A complete listing is available at <http://www.xe.net/gen/iso4217.htm>.
- Other useful devices are the pipe (|), located to the left of the backspace arrow key on most keyboards, and a series of asterisks or hyphens used as graphic devices to separate groups or to highlight headings.
- Remember that e-mail communication cannot be as secure and confidential as the normal postal channel (snail mail).
- Avoid sending large files as attachments—more efficient means are available to transfer such files.

Bibliography

Brittney L. 2000
E-mail and Business Letter Writing: a best-practice approach
London: Foulsham. 192 pp.

Littlejohn A. 2000
Company to Company: a communicative approach to business correspondence in English, 3rd edn
Cambridge, UK: Cambridge University Press. 126 pp.

Sealy J. 1998
The Oxford Guide to Writing and Speaking
Oxford, UK: Oxford University Press. 304 pp.

Chapter **9** Remote control

Chapter 10 at a glance

Length of presentation
Constraints to visibility
Screen presentation, slide projector, or overhead projector?
- Overhead transparencies
- 35-millimetre slides
- PC-based presentations

Templates for transparencies, slides, and screen shows
- Aspect ratio
- Template for overhead transparencies
- Template for PowerPoint-based presentations
- Template for 35-millimetre slides

Bibliography

10 ▶ Stand and deliver

making effective presentations

So far, this handbook has focused on the printed word: headings, lists, abbreviations, tables, references, and so on. It is assumed that your readers will read what you have written at their own pace. They may choose to skim through the document, stopping wherever they find something that interests them, or they may settle down for a close reading. No matter how and what they read, that reading will be a solitary activity, not a group session—the reader is in total control. Presentations, however, are a different matter altogether: the purpose is to effectively communicate ideas or concepts, with just enough data to back them up, and the pace is set by the presenter. A reader may pause to digest the argument or go back a few pages to refresh his or her memory or skip ahead to read the conclusion—a member of the audience has no such options. If you keep this in mind and organize your presentation accordingly, you are well on your way to making it effective. This chapter merely offers some technical hints and tips.

Perhaps the most important ingredient of successful presentations is enthusiasm. If the speaker is excited about the topic, that energy and enthusiasm affect the audience. Body language, voice modulation, and dress are some more important components of effective presentations. All can be mastered with practice. The purpose of this chapter is to address such questions as those listed here.

▶ Which colour combinations work well on computer monitors?
▶ What is the minimum font size for text on overhead transparencies?
▶ How should charts be designed differently for a research paper and for a presentation?
▶ When to use overhead transparencies, 35-mm slides, and computer-based presentations?
▶ When should handouts be distributed: before a talk or after?

> You must consider when to hand out the handout, and how to distribute it. If you pass them out before your talk, people will read ahead, and they may read instead of listening. This upfront distribution usually works best if your handout just provides a framework on which the listeners can take notes. If you are distributing your handout at the end of the talk, it can be more detailed. ⋯ One effective way to control the timing of the handout distribution is to put the material in envelopes which are taped under the chair prior to the audience's arrival.
>
> Walters D E and Walters G C. 2002. *Scientists Must Speak: bringing presentations to life*, pp. 48–49.
> London: Routledge. 132 pp.

Address: http://tejas.serc.iisc.ernet.in/currsci/oct25/articles1.htm

> What indeed constitutes a minimum requirement for an effective scientific presentation? Undoubtedly, the speaker must know what he or she is talking about, an obvious requirement but one that does not always seem to be fulfilled. With slides and transparencies now being the norm, the least that one can demand is that these are legible. ⋯ we now have lectures packed with slides or overheads, some containing so much material ('busy' is a curiously American description), that an audience is soon benumbed into stupefaction. At the other extreme are the 'corporate scientists' with PowerPoint presentations, bewildering for their varied colour backgrounds, but generally devoid of data and confined to well-know generalities.
>
> Balram P. 1999. [editorial] Presenting science. *Current Science* 77: 1005–1006

Address: www.wired.com/wired/archive/11.09/ppt2.html

> Presentations largely stand or fall on the quality, relevance, and integrity of the content. If your numbers are boring, then you've got the wrong numbers. If your words or images are not on point, making them dance in color won't make them relevant. Audience boredom is usually a content failure, not a decoration failure.
>
> Tufte E. 2003. PowerPoint is evil. *Wired* 11 (9)

Length of presentation

It is best to keep the presentation short; 20 minutes is usually adequate. Anything longer, and you stand a greater risk of losing the impact of your presentation. In small groups, with more participation from the audience, you may speak longer whereas formal presentations to large audiences would be shorter.

Restrict the amount of information – collection of facts – you offer; focus more on explaining, demonstrating, or motivating. Aim at giving the whole picture; details are best conveyed through handouts or references to other sources. Resist the temptation to present all the data you have collected; present what is noteworthy.

Constraints to visibility

Sheer quantity of information is the single most common cause of illegible slides or overhead transparencies or screen displays. Accept the large font size required to ensure legibility as given, and trim the contents accordingly, instead of taking the amount of information you would like to put in one slide as given and progressively reducing the font size to accommodate that amount.

Showing slides that are not clearly visible to all reduces the impact of your presentation in two ways. First, it makes you appear inconsiderate; it gives the impression that you have not taken the trouble to make your message clearly visible, and the audience may well grudge you their attention. Second, the section of the audience to whom the slides are not clearly visible soon becomes restive; its members may then begin talking amongst themselves and end up diverting the audience's attention away from your presentation.

Screen presentation, slide projector, or overhead projector?

It is common in technical presentations to use charts, drawings, photographs, lists of bullet points, etc. to supplement the

Chapter **10** Stand and deliver

| Address | http://www2.cddc.vt.edu/ultibase/Articles/dec96/slaug2.html |

Quote

Inappropriate uses of the OHP
When you need to project an image in full colour the OHP can be used, but it is expensive to produce full colour photographic transparencies. It is better to use the 35-mm slide projector which is designed to project photographic images.
> Slaughter T. 1996. A university teacher's guide to overhead projection. [Academic Development Unit, La Trobe University, Australia]

| Address | www.rsvisual.co.uk/support/presentations.htm#selecting |

Quote

Selecting the correct visual aids
If you are presenting to a group of up to six people, visual aids of A3 size will enable your audience to see properly. ··· However, as numbers go up, the size of your visual aid needs to increase proportionately. A flipchart may work for a group of up to ten, but once numbers require auditorium-style seating, you may need a projector.
Interactive sessions are more difficult with a very large group because it is not easy to establish the personal contact that helps elicit response from individuals. In this situation an overhead projector would be essential!
- Can your audience get more from your presentation by participating?
- Is your group a size that is practical to us this method?
- Do you need audience feedback to follow-up after your presentation?

> [Excerpts from the FAQ page of the web site of RSVP, a London-based firm]

talk. Such adjuncts not only add variety but often are essential to the presentation. All can be presented in any of the formats, namely as overhead transparencies, slides, or screen presentations (PowerPoint and similar packages).

Overhead transparencies work best in small groups and in informal settings; 35-mm slides are more formal, require to be prepared well in advance, and are suited to large halls with good projection facilities; screen presentations using a PC are somewhat in between. Slides are undoubtedly superior when it comes to projecting photographs and have the greatest visual impact whereas PC-based presentations permit animations and such enhancements as audio and video clips.

Some reminders about the use of each are given here in the form of lists and are followed by sample specifications for each format and some hints on using them effectively.

Overhead transparencies

- Easy to make new transparencies or to modify existing ones
- Do not require a room to be darkened
- Simple to operate and can be revealed progressively
- Speaker can see the original image easily (unlike the slides in a projector)
- Better results with text and simple line drawings and charts; photographs do not project well
- Colours do not project well; most appear washed out because the ink is not dense enough and the light is very bright (unless you use special type of transparencies)
- Restricted more or less to flat, small, and opaque objects

35-millimetre slides

- Work well in formal settings, especially in large halls with good projection equipment
- Need to be prepared well in advance; cannot be modified at the last moment
- All images, including photographs, project well

| Address | www.conceptron.com/articles/pdf/legibility_of_projected_information.pdf |

> The smallest object that a normal human eye can discern subtends 1 minute of arc (1/60 of a degree) on the retina of the viewer. Empirical studies have shown that, for legibility, the height of a lower case character must subtend at least 10 minutes of arc. As the eye moves off-axis (important to note, since most presentations involve groups of people), this figure needs to be increased. In fact, the ANSI standard calls for a minimum of 16 minutes of arc, and recommends 20 to 22 ···
>
> Musgrave G. 2001. *Legibility of projected information*, p. 3. Coquitlam, British Columbia, Canada: Conceptron Associates. 4 pp.

> 1. Thou shalt keep the design of visuals simple.
> 2. Thou shalt ensure legibility to the person sitting the farthest from the screen.
> 3. Thou shalt use colour with purpose.
> 4. Thou shalt keep special effects (e.g. animations) to a minimum and let content drive their use.
> 5. Thou shalt provide reasonable production deadlines.
> 6. Thou shalt rehearse, rehearse, rehearse before the presentation; during is too late.
> 7. Thou shalt arrive extra early at the presentation site and work closely with the technical professional.
> 8. Thou shalt bring backup visuals.
> 9. Thou shalt project a blank screen during lengthy transitions, while answering audience's questions, or entering into a discussion.
> 10. Thou shalt try to follow 7 of the 10 commandments most of the time.
>
> Zelazny G. 2000. *Say It with Presentations: how to design and deliver successful business presentations*, pp. 30–31. New York: McGraw-Hill. 154 pp.

- Room needs to be darkened
- Fiddly to operate; slides must be loaded correctly if the images are to be the right way around when projected (as one handout puts it, 'There are eight possible ways a slide can be loaded in a projector—seven of them are wrong.')
- Thicker mounts may jam the equipment
- Need to be shown in sequence, with perhaps only a line or two of speech in between (unless you are prepared to talk at length in a darkened room)

PC-based presentations

- Easy to modify even at the last minute (and the changes do not show up as in the case of overhead transparencies)
- Animation and other special effects are possible
- Best suited for small- and medium-sized halls; in larger halls, unless they are darkened, image may look faint
- Easier to depart from the planned script and draw from other available images or files
- Requires more elaborate facilities including appropriate projection equipment with PC-interface, compatible software, and so on
- 'Live' demonstrations of software, web sites, multi-media, etc. possible
- Susceptible to such pitfalls as incompatible versions of software, font substitution, wrong version of the file being saved, and system crash

Templates for transparencies, slides, and screen shows

An image is worth projecting only if it is clearly visible to everybody, including those sitting the farthest from the screen: the longer the distance, the larger the image should be. All images are magnified when they are projected, the extent of magnification being dependent on the focal length of the lens, the distance between the projector and the screen, and so on. However, there are limits to how much an image can be

| Address | www.means-of-escape.com/articles/
03-communication/03-012-viewing.htm |

Quote

It has been found that people with normal (or corrected to normal) vision can reliably resolve a detail that subtends an angle of 1 minute. Using simple geometry, we can work out that the relationship of the observation distance (D) to the detail height (d) for normal sighted people, is given by the relationship tan 1 minute = d/D. This gives D = 3437.75 d.

The height of the alphabet letter E (h) has five details to resolve, i.e. three lines and two spaces so, for normal sighted people, the letter E will be reliably resolved when D = 3437.75 h/5, i.e. when D = 687.55h. … For good measure, at the time of the first edition of BS 5499, a further safety factor of 2 was introduced to give the famous D = 250 h or for the purists, D = 257.83 h.

Creak J. 1997. Viewing distance. *Means of Escape* 1: 18–22

1 cm.
⟵⟶.

Overhead transparencies

2 cm
3.5 cm

- Top margin 60 mm; bottom, 67 mm . . . ↓
- Side margins 20 mm each
- Font: Georgia 24 points
- Interline spacing: 42 points
- Square bullets; no text below bullets
- Main heading indented; 30-point bold
- Subheading 24-point bold, left-aligned
- Maximum 10 lines of text + main heading
- Maximum 45 characters in each line
- All matter within a 17.6 cm by 17.6 cm square

Template

Recommended page set-up in MS Word for A4-size sheets

Rules of thumb to predict visibility

magnified: if the original is small, the projected image is also likely to be too small to be easily visible.

Several elaborate formulas are available to calculate the minimum size of lettering and line widths for easy visibility. One rough indicator is that if you can read a 35-mm slide when it is held at an arm's length or an overhead transparency when it is lying on the floor and you are standing up, it would be clearly visible when projected.

However, it is not enough to merely make the letters large. Imagine a sign painted in large letters but in blue, against a black background: its visibility will be poor because the contrast between the image and its background is poor. Other factors include shape, style, case (capital letters or small letters), the empty space between lines of text, and the overall 'aspect ratio' (height:width) of the whole image.

The templates shown in this chapter take into account all such relevant factors. If you use the templates without any change, you can rest assured that what you project has the best chance of being clearly visible to everybody in your audience. However, as explained in the beginning of this chapter, this is possible only when you are willing to limit the amount of information you want to project at any one time—more than anything else, it is this willingness to present information in small doses that ensures legibility.

Aspect ratio

Keep the overall proportions of the medium in mind. For overhead transparencies, use a square format. For screen shows (including PowerPoint and for preparing visuals for the TV), use a near-square format (3 units tall and 4 units wide). For 35-mm slides, use a landscape format (2 units tall and 3 units wide).

Template for overhead transparencies

Though blank acetate sheets (overhead transparencies) come in A4 size, the transparent area on the overhead projector is more a square than a rectangle. Therefore, keep the matter on every

| Address | www.civil.uwaterloo.ca/pages/undergrad/oral_presentations.pdf | Quote |

Advice
On average, expect to be able to present only 1 overhead per minute.

Your audience should be able to assimilate the information on each overhead within 5-10 seconds. Therefore, keep the text size large enough to be read easily, keep diagrams, maps, etc. simple, and have no more than 3 or 4 key points per overhead.

5.6 cm   2.1 cm

↔ **Title: Georgia Bold 32 points**

2.8 cm

- **First line here (Georgia Bold 28 points)**
- **Second line (line spacing = 56 points)**
- **Square bullets; 1 space after bullet**
- **Bright yellow on deep blue**
- **Phrases, not complete sentences**
- **Minimum text; thick lines, bold letters**
- **Seven lines of text + 1 line of heading**

Template

Recommended settings for PowerPoint presentation

sheet confined to a square box 17.8 cm wide and 17.8 cm tall. Set the text in 24-point Georgia with a line-spacing of 42 points.

Remember to face the audience. If the transparency is mostly text, allow the audience some time to read it. Stop speaking at that time; if you continue speaking, the audience can neither read nor listen. This spell of silence need not be long; about 10 seconds is long enough. In writing text for presentations, use bullet points; do not use complete sentences.

Template for PowerPoint-based presentations

Matter for screen shows is usually in a square format but it is not a perfect square: the default proportion is 3:4, the exact dimensions being 18 cm tall and 24 cm wide.

PowerPoint has many features to enhance the impact of a presentation. Some are functionally useful. For instance, progressive disclosure is possible by displaying bullet points one at a time; as each new point is displayed, the previous one is dimmed. However, it is tempting to turn this into a gimmick by choosing such options as 'Fly from Left' or 'Dissolve', accompanied by such sound effects as shattering of glass or an applause—decide whether you want the audience to remember the contents of your presentation or only its style and choose the features accordingly.

Bright images against a dark background work well with screen presentations. Yellow on deep blue is a particularly effective combination.

As you introduce more colours, it becomes increasingly difficult for viewers to distinguish between them. If you are using dark blue as the background colour and bright yellow as the main colour (particularly recommended), use orange, bright green, and pale blue as additional colours, in that order.

Though PowerPoint presentations have the advantage of portability, remember such constraints as file size, compatible versions, and the possibility of font substitution. It is safer to carry or send the fonts too or embed them in the 'Save as' option.

Chapter **10** Stand and deliver

| Address | http://www.fastcompany.com/online/07/124present.html | Quote |

'And be sure to end by making eye contact with someone who's not the questioner,' she adds. 'That's counterintuitive; people want to answer directly and say, "Did I answer your question?" But you may be encouraging an ongoing exchange with that person.
    Matson E. 1997. Now that we have your complete attention ···. *Fast Company* 7: 124—.

| Address | www.howto4u.com/ | Quote |

Hold a hand-held microphone like you hold an ice cream cone and about one inch from your mouth. ... Hold the microphone perpendicular to your body rather than parallel. Point the corded end at the audience rather than at the floor. Speak into the top of the of the microphone rather than into the side. Your voice will be more audible and much fuller.
    Noyes J. 2002. How to use a hand-held microphone [training tip]. *The Howto4u Workshop Newsletter* 112 (May 2002)

··· to appear at a meeting without PowerPoint would be unwelcome and vaguely pretentious, like wearing no shoes. In darkened rooms at industrial plants and ad agencies, at sales pitches and conferences, this is how people are communicating: no paragraphs, no pronouns—the world condensed into a few upbeat slides, with seven or so words on a line, seven or so lines on a slide. ···
    'But now we've highly paid people sitting there formatting slides – spending hours formatting slides – because it's more fun to do that than concentrate on what you're going to say. ··· Millions of executives around the world are sitting there going, "Arial? Times Roman? Twenty-four point? Eighteen point?"
    Parker I. 2001. Absolute powerpoint: can a software edit our thoughts? *The New Yorker* 77 (13): 76–88

Template for 35-millimetre slides

Slides are the best option if your presentation includes many photographs: it is technically possible to scan them and incorporate the files into a PowerPoint document, but the image cannot be as sharp and colours may change slightly. The overall impact of slides is far greater than screen shows. Also, slide projectors, though not as common as overhead projectors, are more common than computerized projection facilities.

You can also compose the slides in PowerPoint and take a 'printout' on film, to be mounted as for 35-mm slides. This works particularly well for charts and maps, with dense, even colour and high resolution. Remember that 35-mm slides are in 'landscape' format, and the overall proportions are 2:3. In PowerPoint, under File – Page Setup, choose '35mm Slides' instead of the default 'On-screen Show'. If you choose 'On-screen Show', the proportions are changed to 3:4.

For charts, remember to make the lines thick; make the ticks point out; and place axis labels as recommended in Chapter 7. Label the lines or bars or segments directly instead of choosing a legend.

Bibliography

Fowler S L and Stanwick V R. 1995
The GUI Style Guide
Cambridge, Massachusetts, USA: Academic Press (AP Professional). 407 pp.

Rabb M Y. 1993
The Presentation Design Book: tips, techniques & advice for creating effective, attractive slides, overheads, multimedia presentations, screen shows & more,
2nd edn
Chapel Hill, North Carolina, USA: Ventana Press. 346 pp.

Reynolds L and Simmonds D. 1984
Presentation of Data in Science
Dordrecht, The Netherlands: Martinus Nijhoff. 209 pp.

Holcombe M W and Stein J K. 1996
Presentations for Decision Makers, 3rd edn
New York: Van Nostrand. 322 pp.

Chapter 11 at a glance

Planning a poster presentation
Size and layout of a poster
Transport, mounting, and display of posters
> A few other tips on handling poster sessions

11 Research on display
designing effective posters

Though it would take a chapter to describe what an effective poster is and how to design one, a poor poster is described easily enough—physically enlarged version of a research paper, set out in traditional IMRAD sequence (introduction, materials and methods, results and discussion), complete with tables and references. It makes no allowance for the fact that whereas a research paper is meant to convey information, a poster is meant to attract attention and stimulate discussion, often of the very latest findings (which may be preliminary). Research papers are *read*, the readers usually working alone at their desks, whereas posters are *displayed*, usually at the venue of a conference, the viewers often standing at least a metre away.

This chapter offers guidance on preparing effective posters: posters that capture attention, present findings quickly, and interest viewers in the subject. The chapter seeks to answer questions such as those listed below.

- How should one plan for a poster presentation?
- What is the usual size for a poster?
- Which is a good font for posters?
- What is the smallest clearly visible point size?
- How can one transport large posters?

Planning a poster presentation

Perhaps surprisingly, preparing an effective poster requires far more planning than that required for a research paper. A poster must draw and hold attention and generate interest. An effective poster tells a story, and tells it concisely. Planning for a poster is like distillation—you must extract the essence and discard everything else.

In general, details of the method and references are best supplied in a handout: let the poster contain only the essentials. Pretend that you are using a picture postcard to tell your

| Address | www.tss.uoguelph.ca/TGuides/EPDfinal.pdf | Quote |

At poster sessions there is intense competition for audience attention. In their first 3 seconds your audience will determine whether to stay and explore your content or leave. If they stay you have 30 seconds to secure their attention by conveying an overall understanding of your subject matter.
   Teaching Support Services, University of Guelph. Effective poster design: a step by step guide, p. 1. Guelph, Ontario, Canada: University of Guelph. 13 pp.

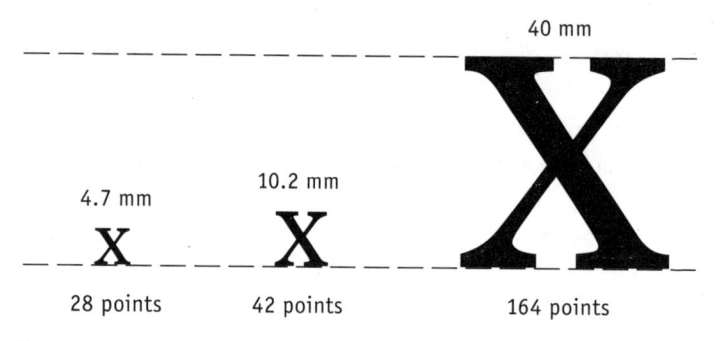

			Example
4.7 mm	10.2 mm	40 mm	
x	x	X	
28 points	42 points	164 points	

Figure 1 Height of Georgia lower-case 'x' in three font-sizes (actual size)

friends about your research. Allow yourself no more than 80 words. Identify the most important finding: if it answers a question, use the question for a title or heading. Think how you could present the findings with pictures—including cartoons, graphs, and flow charts. Think whether the poster could include any exhibits (samples, scale models, etc.) to supplement its message.

Once this material has been assembled, devise a suitable title. It could be a question or a statement but it must be brief (12 or fewer words), self-explanatory, and convey unambiguously what the poster is all about.

Size and layout of a poster

Organizers will specify the orientation (horizontal or vertical) and the exact size: A1, which is 8 times the size of A4, is common in Europe and a 4 × 6 feet poster board in the US. A1 is 594 × 841 mm (approximately 23½ × 33 inches). It is possible to design the poster in a graphics software such as AutoCAD or CorelDraw, which allows the entire poster of that size to be printed in one piece and also in miniature, which makes effective handouts. However, such files are large and take a long time to print. Also, such one-piece posters are not easy to handle and transport; it is better to divide the poster into 4 or 8 parts, each to be printed on an A3 or A4 sheet, and then assemble the poster on site. Increasingly, they are rolled and carried in standard plastic tubes, which protect them well.

Keep the text to a minimum but set it in a generous font size: 28-point Georgia is recommended. A small (lower-case) 'x' at this size is 4.7 mm tall. For headings, use 42-point Georgia (x-height = 10.2 mm). Use a line spacing of 56 points. Set the title of the poster in 164-point Georgia (x-height = 40 mm). Figure 1 shows actual sizes of letters. The points covered in Chapter 10, on presentations, are equally relevant to preparing effective posters.

Arrange the layout to guide the eye as the story unfolds. Link the visuals (photographs, charts, etc.) and text clearly to

> By the time you reach your destination, your poster can be in a sorry state. Photographs may have become unstuck and other sheets may be annoyingly unwilling to go flat again. ⋯ The single large photographic print sounds ideal but is usually expensive. We advocate using a sheet of mounting card that will fit into a suitcase or can be wrapped and carried under the arm. For this reason we believe the A3 modular system to be the most practical. Using this modular technique our data can be printed on A4 sheets of coloured paper, these can be fixed to the card with spray glue, and the result can be effective and inexpensive.
>
>   Simmonds D and Reynolds L. 1994. *Data Presentation and Visual Literacy in Medicine and Science*, pp. 132–133. Oxford, UK: Butterworth-Heinemann. 192 pp.

Address: www.medsci.uu.se/occmed/poster/faq/default.htm

> Remember to take your poster, preferably with you personally. This means taking it as carry-on luggage if you fly. If you can, take a copy of your poster on diskette or on your laptop computer. Take a back-up copy of your poster in your suitcase. Pins and tape can be good to have along since you can't be sure that the conference organizers will provide you with these materials.
>
>   Carter N and Nilsson K. 2001. The poster site: frequently asked questions. [University of Uppsala, Sweden]

Address: www.biology.lsa.umich.edu/research/labs/ktosney/file/PostersHome.html

> A poster is not just a standard research paper stuck to a board. An effective poster uses a different, visual grammar. It shows, not tells. It expresses your points in graphical terms. It avoids visual chaos, with many jagged edges or various-sized boards that distract the viewer. Instead, it guides the viewer by using a visual logic, with an hierarchical structure that emphasizes the main points. It displays the essential content – the messages – in the title, main headings, and graphics. ⋯ All elements, even the figure legends, are visible from 4 feet away.
>
>   Tosney K. 2000. How to create a poster that graphically communicates your message

each other. Empty spaces are not out of place; avoid the temptation to fill every square centimetre of space, but remember that posters do not require generous margins—unlike printed documents, posters are not bound or annotated. Observe the layout of posters in good museums. Large advertisements in newspapers or quality magazines are another source of ideas on effective layouts—much time and money will have gone into them.

Colour heightens the impact of a poster although too many colours make it look disorganized. For large areas of colour, use coloured paper. Coloured paper ensures stable and uniform colour whereas colour plotters or laser printers may introduce streaks and patches and the colour may run or rub off. If possible, have the entire poster or its constituent parts laminated; matt lamination is better than glossy lamination because it prevents glare or dazzle.

Transport, mounting, and display of posters

Never fold any part of a poster; folding introduces more or less permanent creases and may crack the lamination. Avoid large sheets; as a last resort, they can be rolled and packed in tubes of plastic or stiff cardboard.

A few other tips on handling poster sessions

- Include a miniature poster as a part of your handout; it will also help in assembling the poster at the site.
- Carry an assortment of mounting materials. Drawing pins, double-sided sticky tape, hook-and-loop fasteners ('Velcro'), and large clips are some of the options for mounting posters. The most suitable method depends on the surface on which the poster is to be mounted. Though organizers usually offer to make available all necessary materials, it is better to carry your own supplies.
- Also carry scissors, a small hammer, pliers, and a length of string. (Do not carry wire: you may be suspected of carrying a bomb!)

Chapter **11** Research on display

| Address | www.asp.org/education/Howto_onPosters.html#part4 | Quote |

We strongly recommend that you write up a brief hand-out to accompany your poster. This will allow you to provide a little more detail about your work (though it isn't meant as an opportunity to author a full paper on the topic) and will also achieve the important goal of sending your audience away with your work and your name in hand. The ideal handout is just one to three pages long, with all of the important points of your talk in both text and graphics. An envelope of these can be attached to your poster display area so that your colleagues can easily collect them.

Miller L, Christine J, and Ann A. 2000. Expanded guidelines for giving a poster presentation.

Removing and saving the poster
In many cases, other poster sessions follow yours or other activities are planned for the poster room, so it is essential (and prudent, if you don't want to lose the poster!) to take it down promptly at the designated time. ··· 'Used' posters are nice to save for display at the home institution—outside your office or lab, for example, to inform (impress) visitors, colleagues, and future co-workers about your productivity and accomplishments.

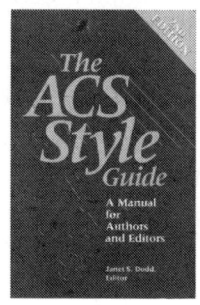

Schowen K B. 1977. Tips for effective poster presentations, in *The ACS Style Guide: a manual for authors and editors*, 2nd edn, p. 38, edited by J S Dodd. Washington, DC: American Chemical Society. 460 pp.

- If appropriate, display the title of the session, venue, and the time of your presentation near the poster.
- Provide 'take away' copies of the handout and display them prominently near the poster. If possible, keep a stack of your business cards handy or pin a card to each handout. Make sure your card shows your e-mail address.
- Request visitors to leave their business cards and provide a receptacle for the purpose.
- Never leave your poster unattended; be available for discussion. If this is impossible, be sure to put your photograph on the poster so readers will recognize you elsewhere.
- Bring your own conference badge with your name in large print; badges supplied by organizers are sometimes illegible.

Chapter 12 at a glance

Preparing a publication-friendly manuscript
 ▸ Tips on preparing printouts or hard copies for submission

The covering letter

Packing and dispatch

Preparing electronic files

File management
 ▸ Footnotes
 ▸ Formatting
 ▸ Tables and figures

Labelling and dispatching electronic files

12 ▶ Publish or perish
submitting manuscripts to journals

Submitting papers for publication is a competitive business. Reputable journals always have a pile of manuscripts cleared by the journal's reviewers and waiting to be published. When all papers in that pile are more or less of equal importance, how can you ensure that your paper has the best chance of being picked up first? The manuscript of a typical research paper is launched on a long journey from the moment it leaves its author, a voyage that culminates in its final appearance as a published paper. This chapter offers some tips on how to make that journey faster and smoother and offers answers to some frequently asked questions including the following.

- Which is the preferred format for submitting a manuscript to a journal, a printout or an electronic copy?
- Why is it better to keep tables and figures separate from the main text?
- How should electronic files be labelled?
- What information should the covering letter contain?
- Where should the footnotes go in electronic copy?

Please note that most academic journals routinely receive unsolicited manuscripts of research papers and are adequately geared to handle them. Magazines and trade journals are different: you will save a great deal of time and effort by sending a preliminary proposal to the editor of the magazine briefly describing the article you intend to write and your qualifications to do so. Much of the advice that follows is intended for researchers who intend to submit their manuscripts to academic journals.

Preparing a publication-friendly manuscript
Baggage handlers at airports can give you helpful tips about packing: because they are familiar with the process, their advice

> Neatness counts. Nothing will turn an editor off faster than a manuscript that is sloppy, poorly typed, or single-spaced. The goal is to make your ··· manuscript as editor-friendly as possible—if your reader has to squint, turn the page to an odd angle, or wade through illegible material, you've already given him or her reason to reject your work. While this may sound harsh, it is a realistic reflection of the enormous amount of material an editor must read ··· 
>
> Mehren J v. 1993. What editors look for in a query letter, proposal, and manuscript, p. 95, in *Editors on Editing: what writers need to know about what editors do*, 3rd edn, edited by G Gross. New York: Grove Press. 377 pp.

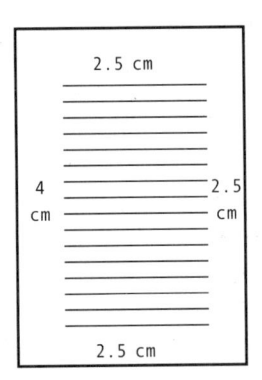

Type everything in double-spacing with ample margins all around.

Fasten all pages securely together using bulldog clips or large paper clips; avoid stapling the pages.

Margins and line spacing

is practical. So with publishing: knowing what happens to manuscripts helps you to prepare them (and their electronic versions) so that they not only survive the publishing process but emerge in good shape.

At least half a dozen people work on any manuscript, often for long hours, and each of them handles dozens or even hundreds of manuscripts. Some read it in detail, from the title to every comma within the text. Copy editors need space in which to mark their questions, revisions, and instructions to typesetters and designers — hence the insistence on double-spaced manuscripts. Others may give the text a cursory glance but record such details as the number of pages, illustrations if any, the author's address, and so on. Yet others may photocopy parts of it, remove some pages and fax them, stamp some pages, and write instructions for other handlers. The manuscript must be so prepared as to make these jobs easy.

Most journals prefer to receive hard copies in the first instance. Electronic forms are requested only after a paper is finally accepted, after it has been revised as suggested by the reviewers and required by the editor. However, check the latest 'instructions to authors' issued by the journal. Here are some useful tips for preparing a manuscript.

Tips on preparing printouts or hard copies for submission

- Use 11- or 12-point characters *throughout*. Print no part of the manuscript in type smaller than 11 points.
- Leave enough space between the lines of all text, including abstracts, tables, and references. A line spacing of at least 17 points – lines 6 mm apart – is essential but 34 points (approximately 8.5 mm apart) is recommended, which is sometimes referred to as double spacing (3 lines to the inch).
- Leave ample margins all around: at least 4 cm to the left and at least 2.5 cm at the top, right, and bottom.
- Fasten all pages securely together. Mere stapling is seldom adequate; single sheets, especially the last page or two, often come adrift and will be lost: use bulldog clips or large paper clips.

Chapter **12** Publish or perish

Set the text in a single column; do not attempt to make the manuscript look like a published paper.

Mechanics of preparing manuscripts

- Do not format the text into columns, no matter how it is formatted in the printed journal. You do not have to use the same font but try to match the style for headings, tables, figure captions, and so on. For instance, if the journal prints the title in bold, print the title of the paper in bold; if the journal prints the address in italics, print it in italics, and so on. Omit background shading, sometimes used in tables or figures: the publisher will insert such touches at the appropriate stage.
- Print all text and drawings in dense black with clear, sharp edges on good-quality white paper. Do not use fan-fold paper, onion-skin or airmail paper. Print only on one side.
- The ink used in ink-jet printers is water soluble and may run: use a laser printer or submit a good photocopy.
- Number all pages and display the page number prominently.
- Include page headers (a shortened version of the title of the paper) but do not include any identifying information such as your name or affiliation when submitting manuscripts to peer-reviewed or refereed journals.
- Add the identifying information (name and affiliation) in a header or footer when submitting articles to newspapers and magazines.
- Send complete manuscripts, including *everything*: title page, contents or abstracts as appropriate, the text, tables, figures, references, photographs, drawings, logos, whatever—everything that you want to appear in print. However, do not send original photographs in the first instance; send them only when the journal asks for them.
- Attach a list of tables and figures.
- Send the required number of copies.
- Give all the necessary information for contacting you: your mailing address, fax and telephone, e-mail, and so on. If you expect to be away, give the dates and contact details or identify someone authorized to handle proofs, etc.
- Comply with any other instructions given by the journal or the publisher. In particular, follow the exact style of the

It is reasonable to ask for feedback if you have not heard from the editors within 12 weeks. When my organization, the Buckingham Consortium, was asked to create an electronic manuscript tracking system for editors within MCB University Press we asked a core group of editors to identify the vulnerabilities in their own systems. Not hearing back from reviewers swiftly enough was one; not hearing back from authors with their revisions was another. It therefore may be prudent to gently remind the editor that you are still awaiting feedback. The message might prompt the editor to remind the reviewer and therefore help nudge the manuscript along.

Day A. 1996. *How to Get Research Published in Journals*, p. 118. Aldershot, UK: Gower. 142 pp.

journal in formatting references. Chapter 8 of this handbook gives more information on formatting references.

The covering letter

A carefully prepared manuscript creates a favourable impression but the first thing that a journal editor is likely to see is the covering letter. Make it brief but draw the editor's attention to its significance. A few points to keep in mind are listed below.

- Address the covering letter, by name, to the editor. Follow the instructions to authors that appear in a recent issue of the target journal.
- If the journal has different 'departments', such as short communications, letters to the editor, and book reviews in addition to full papers, indicate the category under which your manuscript is to be considered.
- Briefly indicate the significance of your research and its suitability to that journal.
- Give legal release. A commonly used phrasing is as follows: 'Enclosed is my manuscript titled . . . , which I am submitting for publication in . . .' Such a release allows the editor to send it for reviewing though it is your confidential property; do not just say 'Enclosed is my manuscript' because this does not authorize the editor to show it to anyone.
- Mention the details of any accompanying matter, especially photographs or 35-mm slides.
- Give the total number of words when submitting articles to magazines or newspapers, where space is an important consideration. Mention how you are particularly qualified to write on the topic.
- If you expect to be away from your place of work for spells longer than a couple of days after submitting a manuscript, indicate that in the covering letter and mention how you may be contacted while away from your office. Repeat this information, as mentioned earlier, in the manuscript as well as a part of your contact details.

| Address | www.ag.iastate.edu/journals/rie/hows.htm | Quote |

How long to wait for results
Contact the editor after six months
- Editors do not have an alarm clock that goes off for each paper after a certain period of time has elapsed.
- If it has been six months from the date of acknowledgment, you should contact the editor.
- If you are counting from the date of your submission, allow seven months. ···
- If you do not get a response within two months, send a second inquiry.

Choi K. 2002. How to publish in top journals

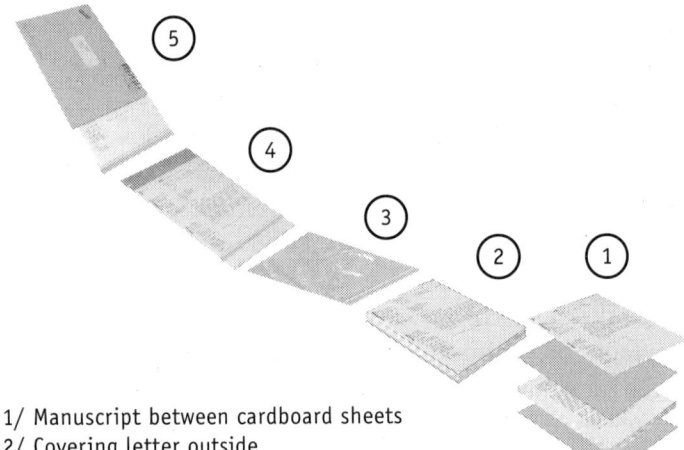

1/ Manuscript between cardboard sheets
2/ Covering letter outside
3/ Polythene bag
4/ Manuscript inside a polythene bag; covering letter visible through the bag
5/ The entire assembly within the mailing envelope

Assembling a manuscript for dispatch

Packing and dispatch

Careful preparation of manuscripts extends to packing and dispatch, and here are a few proven tips.

- Always keep the pages flat; do not fold or roll them.
- Never attach photographs to the manuscript with a paper clip: it can leave a permanent mark on the photograph. Put photographs in a separate envelope and insert a blank sheet between every two photographs. Attach this envelope securely to the rest of the manuscript.
- Use envelopes of stiff cardboard for mailing. If these are not available, use two sheets of cardboard cut to size, or any thin and rigid cardboard box, to protect the manuscript. Place the covering letter *outside* the cardboard sheets and then put the entire assembly within a polythene bag, especially if you are sending it out in the rainy season. The polythene bag goes inside the mailing envelope; use a cloth-backed one if possible.
- Avoid sending manuscripts by post during the festive season, for instance during Diwali or Christmas, when postal services are overloaded.

Preparing electronic files

Once a manuscript is accepted, you will probably be asked to supply the final version on paper with a matching disk file. If disk files are prepared wisely, they make life easy for publishers; if not, they are potentially the richest source of costly mishaps. Understandably, most publishers will simply discard them and instruct the author to send a fresh disk or have the text keyed in again, with all the attendant delays and problems.

Simplicity is the key to efficient transfer of electronic manuscripts. Elaborate formatting of such files only adds to problems because all large publishers use sophisticated, custom-designed software: word-processing packages such as Word or WordPerfect are fine for authors, but publishers often use custom-made programs or such off-the-shelf page layout programs as QuarkXPress or PageMaker.

Chapter **12** Publish or perish

> Quote
>
> - Use a minimum of formatting. Most formatting must be removed before typesetting, and this is time-consuming if it is not possible to do so globally. Superscripts are acceptable for notes, however.
> - Leave text unjustified.
> - Turn off your word processor's automatic hyphenation feature. The only hyphens that should appear should be in compound words.
>
> University of Toronto Press. *Author Handbook*
> <www.utpress.utoronto.ca/editorial/msprep.html#disks>

> Quote
>
> | Address | www.uncpress.unc.edu/stet/2.html#electronictext |
>
> Preparing the electronic text
> 1. Prepare your manuscript on the same system – both hardware and software – from start to finish.
> 2. Create a new file for each chapter or other major subdivision of the book and name the files sequentially: intro, chap1, chap2, etc. Front matter, bibliography, and other apparatus should be in separate files. It is fine to split a long chapter into two files, but please do not combine two or more chapters into one file. In particular, never put the entire manuscript in a single file, which may be impossible for us to convert.
>
> University of North Carolina Press. 2002. *Stet: a handbook for authors*

First, work on the version that you intend to use to take the printout. This will have been formatted so as to yield a printout that matches the target journal's style, especially for references, headings, and captions.

Make all the required changes in that version; only when it is final, down to the last comma, should you start preparing the electronic version. If possible, generate a version of the final document in PDF (portable document format) at this stage. A file with a .pdf extension is the electronic equivalent of a print version and reproduces it faithfully. Open the PDF file with Acrobat Reader and make sure that it matches with the printout. Pay particular attention to special characters such as Greek letters or unusual symbols. A useful source of information on creating PDF files is <fastlane.nsf.gov/a1/pdfcreat.htm>.

In a nutshell, preparing the electronic version amounts to stripping away virtually all the formatting: about the only items you should retain are bold, italics, hard returns (Enters), and tab stops. The following instructions will increase your chances of preparing acceptable electronic files that interface smoothly with virtually all software packages used in publishing.

File management

- As the first step, break the file into many files. If you have integrated tables and figures into the text in the formatted version, take them out and make one file for all the tables together and as many files as there are figures.
- You may transfer files across the Internet, but make sure that the file names are indicative of contents and that, as far as possible, the original 3-character extensions of each program (.doc for Word files, .cdr for CorelDraw files, .xls for Excel files, and so on) are retained.
- If you are submitting the manuscript of a whole book on disk, make separate files for 'front matter' (title, preface, foreword, contents, etc.); a file for each of the chapters and one for references; and a file for 'back matter' (glossary, notes, annexes, etc.). Make separate files for tables and

Example

In preparing the final version of the manuscript on disk, remove all special formatting: set the text single-spaced, in Times, without headers, footers, page numbers, visually distinct headings, and so on.

Quote

If a paper is not in the stipulated format of the journal, the copy editor will have to restructure it, which takes a lot of work and runs the risk of distorting the author's meaning. If the copy contains a lot of hand-written revisions, the copy editor will have to either retype those parts or gamble that the printer's compositor can read it. Either route wastes time and increases the potential for errors. Authors, being the most knowledgeable about their papers, are in the best position to make any revisions or changes in format without the introduction of errors or distortion of meaning.

Bishop C T. 1984. *How to Edit a Scientific Journal*. Philadelphia, Pennsylvania, USA: ISI Press. 138 pp.

A 'plain vanilla' file

figures and name the files systematically, so that it will be easy to identify their contents from the file name.
- Send the publisher a short test file but it should be representative of your work in that it should contain samples of figures, tables, special characters used in the text, scanned images if any, and so on. This is particularly recommended for book-length documents.

Footnotes
- If you have used footnotes, prepare a separate file only for the text of the footnotes.

Formatting
- Never use the space bar to make items line up with one another; use tabs.
- If you have used such features as automated bullet lists or numbered lists, remove that formatting. If you have inserted bullet points manually, remove those as well: bullets are not a part of the ASCII character set and may yield a different character when read by another software.
- As far as possible, use only those characters that you can generate with the standard keyboard, starting with the tilde (-) at the top left in most keyboards and ending at the question mark at the bottom right.
- If it is necessary to use special symbols (the degree sign, Greek letters, etc.), highlight them in the printout the first time they occur in the text. Prepare a separate list of such symbols and indicate how you have inserted them and font used (Symbol, Wingdings, WP Typographic Symbols, or whatever).
- Remove headers, footers, line numbers, and page numbers.
- Use the standard default margins and use single spacing and left justification throughout—for every single item in the text from title to the list of references.
- Change the font to Times, the most widely supported font worldwide and across dozens of software packages.

| Address | www.routledge.com/authors/authors.pdf |

Quote

- Each chapter should be saved as a separate file. Do not put all the text into one large file—this is difficult to process and a file error may result, restricting access to the entire text. File sizes should not be more than about 100 K (kilobytes) each— equivalent to no more than around 100 pages of typescript.
- It is not necessary to start a new disk for each file. Depending upon which disk type you use, an average length book usually requires 1–2 disks.
- Make sure your disks contain only the text of your book, and only one copy of each chapter, etc. Erase all redundant files.

Taylor & Francis Books. 2001. *Instructions for Authors*, p. 7. London: Taylor & Francis. 32 pp.

Accurate table conversion is one of the most critical, complex, and laborious aspects of document conversion. A proper representation of a table will include, among other properties, proper cell and row identification, vertical and horizontal alignment, separators, spanning, and differentiation of header and body rows. As with most other aspects of document conversion, what will exist in the source document can vary widely from project to project.

Quote

Gross M. 2003. Data capture and conversion, p. 213 in *The Columbia Guide to Digital Publishing*, edited by W E Kasdorf. New York: Columbia University Press. 750 pp.

- Remove paragraph indents and insert one hard return (Enter) between every two paragraphs: press Enter at the end of a paragraph and press Enter one more time before beginning the next paragraph.
- Similarly, separate each item from the next with only one hard return. For example, press Enter once at the end of a heading and one more time before beginning the text that follows the heading.

Tables and figures

- Format tables carefully. In particular, make sure that only one tab separates one column from the next and that only one hard return separates one row from the next. The table may not look properly set on screen but ignore that; it will come out all right in the end. On the contrary, inserting extra tabs and hard returns in an effort to line up the table properly on screen is counterproductive—it only means extra work at the publisher's end.
- The same considerations apply to graphic files: strip them of all such special effects as shadows, fills, shades, and so on. With charts, supply the numerical data on which the chart is based, especially if you have used a professional drawing program such as CorelDraw, Adobe Illustrator, or Aldus Freehand.
- Supply graphic files in the format specified by the publisher (EPS, TIFF, BMP, and so on).

Labelling and dispatching electronic files

A busy publishing office receives hundreds of disks; most of them probably look alike, except for the label. Make yours easy to identify by clearly marking its origin on the paper label *and* using the 11-character electronic label. If the publisher suggests a particular scheme for labelling, use that. If not, the following tips may prove useful.

- If you are sending only one disk, label it with your name (with initials, if the name is a common one). If the name is longer than 11 letters, use the first 11.

Address	www.andreas.com/faq-disks.html

Don't use a pencil or ball-point pen to write on a disk label. You'll press the dust sleeve inside of the disk case against the disk. The dust will be caked onto the surface of the disk. Much worse, however, is that you'll indent the surface of the disk. Use a felt tip pen and write lightly.

Ramos A. 2000. FAQ: disks, disk drives, and hard disks, an introduction to media storage

Labelling the disk

- If sending more than one disk, shorten the name and ensure that each label not only identifies that disk but also states how many there are. For instance, you could label the first one AKSINGH1OF3, the second one AKSINGH2OF3, and so on. Zip disks and read-write CDs, which can carry large amounts of data, are not only more convenient — a single disk serves the purpose — but also more reliable.
- Use a felt-tipped pen to write the paper label. On the label, supply your name and mailing address and, if possible, the list of files contained in the disk. Specify the software and the version number you have used in preparing the files.
- Pack the disks securely. Use special envelopes or stiff-backed envelopes and protect the disk with bubble wrap.
- Fine out whether you can send the files through the Internet by using FTP (file transfer protocol); enlist the help of your system administrator if there is one.

Chapter 13 at a glance

The purpose of punctuation
Deciding when to use punctuation and what marks to choose
Some common points of style related to punctuation
The serial (or Oxford) comma
References

13 ▶ What is the point?

punctuation for clearer writing

Consider a line of text set without any gaps between words: it is usually possible to decode it but takes longer to do so — each space separates one word from the next and makes the structure of the message clearer. A comma may serve the same purpose, working as a 'thousands separator' – as in 14,250 or 283,567 – and a semicolon is necessary to separate two or more groups of words that already contain commas, as in Jones, Smith, and Crawford 1997; Singh, Chopra, and Gupta 1998; and Das and Sengupta 1999. A full stop separates one sentence from the next, and a first-line indent separates one paragraph from the next.

The purpose of this chapter is to address such questions as the following.
▶ Is it necessary to put a comma in dates? (25 July 1999 or 25 July, 1999?)
▶ What is the default: single quotes ('. . .') or double quotes ("...")?
▶ Should the first letter after a colon be a capital letter?
▶ Which is right: 'a, b, and c' or 'a, b and c'?
▶ If a sentence ends with an endnote or reference number indicated with a superscript character, where does the superscript go: before the full stop or after it?

The purpose of punctuation

One widely held belief is that the purpose of punctuation is to indicate pauses when the matter is to be read aloud. This is partly true in that punctuation does serve to make up for such cues as intonation, pauses, and stress, which are common in speech and help in making the speaker's intended meaning clearer. However, and more important, punctuation helps to make the structure of written text clearer by telling the reader how one set of words, phrases, and clauses relates to another.

> Punctuation probably reached its zenith in the late 19th century, helping to make sense of the then fashionably interminable sentences. Sentences held together by a dozen or more commas, semicolons, brackets and other marks were commonplace. Nowadays sentences, influenced by the brevity of the newspaper style, are shorter, and the need for the complicated division within long sentences has all but disappeared. Commas are freely dropped where the meaning remains unaffected. Stops after abbreviations are disappearing in a general quest for typographic tidiness. The majority of the English-speaking population probably goes through life without ever using, on paper, any punctuation marks other than the comma, dash and full stop.
>
> King G. 2001. *The Times Writer's Guide*, p. 96. Glasgow, UK: HarperCollins. 832 pp.

Address www.calstatela.edu/centers/write_cn/gptips.htm

> These two conceptions of punctuation – to indicate pauses for breathing and for rhetorical effect, and to delineate the grammatical boundaries of the text – are to a certain extent contradictory, opposing the creative, living, breathing, individual voice with an analytical, logical, rule-driven structure. These conceptions co-exist in our society, making punctuation both difficult to teach and confusing to learn. ⋯ John Dawkins, writing in a recent issue of *College Composition and Communication*, advises us to disregard handbook advice on punctuation anyway. ⋯ Dawkins sees the various punctuation marks as encoding different degrees of separation between independent clauses, or between elements in independent clauses. This perspective is different from either the breath-related or the grammatical perspectives already discussed, in that it is based on the writer's perception of the conceptual relationships.
>
> Edlund J R. Breath, grammar, and proper punctuation
>
> [Dawkins J. 1995. Teaching punctuation as a rhetorical tool. *College Composition and Communication* **46**: 533–548]

A colon, for instance, introduces a list; a pair of parentheses tells the reader that the enclosed matter is incidental to the main text; and an apostrophe shows possession.

Deciding when to use punctuation and what marks to choose

In some ways, you learn to use punctuation the same way you learn to use words—by reading a great deal, and particularly by reading effective writers. Patterns of punctuation are thus absorbed unconsciously. However, patterns of punctuation change with time: early texts used virtually no punctuation; texts published in the 19th century were heavily punctuated; and the trend from the late 20th century favours light punctuation. British and American practices sometimes differ. For instance, it is more common in the US to add a colon after the salutation in a business letter whereas the British practice is to use a comma or no punctuation at all. The recommendations in this handbook are based mostly on current British practice.

Usually, as you write and as it becomes clearer to you how words, phrases, and clauses relate to one another, you will find it easy enough to indicate these relationships through appropriate punctuation marks. You can then compare your usage with any authoritative source such as Carey (1958), Trask (1997), or Kirkman (1999). Allen (2002) is a straightforward and simple introduction illustrated with cartoons. It is unlikely that you would learn how to punctuate effectively simply by studying the use of each punctuation mark. Instead, here is a selection of the most frequently used points of style regarding punctuation. The least contentious and easiest to apply are covered first.

Some common points of style related to punctuation

Slash to mark financial years Use a slash with financial years, as in 1998/99 (to mean some months of 1998 and some months of 1999). However, in the case of years at the turn of the

What is the difference between a helix and a spiral? ✓

What is the difference between a helix and a spiral ? ✗

Set the question mark close to the preceding character.

Example

The 'aspect ratio' of a standard TV screen is 3:4 ✓

The 'aspect ratio' of a standard TV screen is 3 : 4 ✗

In ratios, set the quantities on either side close to the colon.

Example

first-hand inter-regional

The *hyphen* joins words or marks a break within a word at the end of a line of text.

Example

The Second World War (1939–45)

The New Delhi – Mumbai Rajdhani Express

This is a technique that stage magicians – at least the best of them – exploit with amazing results.

The *en dash* indicates a range or direction; a pair of en dashes works like brackets.

Biological evolution proceeds by a grand, inexorable process of trial and error—and without the errors, the trials wouldn't accomplish anything.

The *em dash* signals a summing up or abrupt change at the end of a sentence.

Example

Gender inequalities in India tend to be greater than those even in sub-Saharan Africa.[1]

Place footnote marker *after* the full stop.

Example

century, use the 4-digit form of both the years for 1999/2000 and include the leading zero for the next nine years, as in 2000/01, 2001/02, and so on up to 2008/09.

Comma in dates and citations In writing dates, exclude the comma between the month and the year. In references within text using the author–year system, exclude the comma between the author/s and the year. Separate one reference from the next with a comma but use a semicolon if any of the references contains internal commas (as in Das and Sengupta 1999; Jones, Smith, and Crawford 1997; Singh, Chopra, and Gupta 1998).

Space and the question mark Set the question mark close up to the character that comes before it; do not insert a space between the two.

Spaces and the colon Except when used to indicate a ratio, set the colon close to the word that comes before but insert one space after the colon. In ratios, set the numbers on either side of the colon close up (as in 1:1); do *not* insert spaces (as in 1 : 1). A colon cannot end a sentence; therefore, the matter that follows a colon normally does not begin with a capital letter.

Single quotes or double quotes Use single quotes to mark a direct quotation and double quotes to enclose a quote within a quote. Enclose within single quotes uncommon words and words used figuratively or with reservation. Single quotes are also useful for indicating that it is the appearance, sound, or some other property of the matter (words or letters) within the quotes that is being discussed or emphasized and not the meaning (the car traced the path of an 'S'; the 'c' in 'care' is hard but that in 'cease' is soft; the 'e' in the typescript was a blur; and so on).

Reference marks after the full stop Place superscript characters used for indicating endnotes or references *after* the full stop at the end the sentence.

Semicolons to separate items with internal commas In a list of names of people or places, use semicolons to separate one item from the next if two or more items already contain commas (as in Pune, Maharashtra; Indore, Madhya Pradesh; and Bikaner,

> **Colon surgery**
> Don't break up a perfectly good sentence with a colon just because a number of items are about to be listed. Lists need to be preceded with colons only when they are introduced abruptly, with no introduction, or with the following or as follows or here are or something like that. Don't use the colon after the problems include or the members of the task force are.
>
> Walsh B. 2000. *Lapsing into a Comma: a curmudgeon's guide to the many things can go wrong in print—and how to avoid them*, p. 75. Chicago, Illinois, USA: Contemporary Books. 246 pp.

Address	http://folk.uio.no/lynnp/grammartips/ A_dash_to_the_finish.doc

> Sometimes you may want to interrupt a sentence with a parenthetical remark to create emphasis or group logical bits of information together. You can set off a parenthetical remark with a pair of commas, parentheses, or dashes. Commas are the weakest interrupter—that is, the reader tends to read through the parenthetical comment as if it were not set apart. Dashes are a stronger interrupter and call attention to the offset material. Parentheses are the strongest interrupter, so much so that the parenthetical material is not considered important to the sentence at all. (Thus they do not create emphasis.) ··· As a writer, you will often have to think about grouping your parenthetical material either so it stands out better (by using dashes) or does not detract from the main point of the sentence (by using parentheses).
>
> Nygaard L P. 2002. A dash to the finish: style issues for hyphens, en dashes, and em dashes

Rajasthan or Mr Maurice Strong, Executive Coordinator for United Nations Reform; Mr James Gustave Speth, Administrator, UNDP; and Ms Elizabeth Dowdeswell, Executive Director, UNEP).

If only one item in the series contains internal commas, it is not necessary to separate one item from the next with semicolons so long as the item with internal commas is the last one.

Dashes in place of parentheses Use spaced en dashes when – for extra emphasis – you want to use paired dashes in place of brackets, as shown here, but use a *closed-up em dash* to introduce a summary, an abrupt change of direction, or an unexpected conclusion—as in this contrived example.

Lists Punctuation in lists follows a set of conventions: see Chapter 3 for full details.

Punctuation after verbs Do not use a colon or any other punctuation mark immediately after a verb. This simple convention is most frequently violated in sentences that contain lists, as in 'The common causes of illness are: malnutrition, contaminated water, and polluted air' or 'Those present included: the prime minister, chief ministers, and governors'—remove the colon in both sentences.

Apostrophes with decades and plurals Do not use the apostrophe with decades (1990s not 1990's) and plural forms of abbreviations set in all-capitals (MPs, RETs, and FAQs).

Hyphenation Avoid using end-of-the-line hyphenation; in word-processing and page layout programs, this feature can be turned off. These hyphens have a habit of persisting across files and programs. You may have reformatted a document or re-used some text by pasting it into another document. However, hyphens inserted by the program in the original version to mark line-breaks can remain embedded even when the words no longer occur at the ends of lines in the reformatted or new document. Some amusing word-breaks published by the weekly magazine *New Scientist* taken from its own pages include hyphens, not-ice, fun-ding, port-ion, and t-rouble and those from

When all is said, this remains a matter for individual choice. But it is also a matter of general principle; you can belong to the 'final comma school' or the 'no final comma school', but, having made your choice, you should aim at consistency. Because the 'no final comma' principle breaks down now and again through ambiguity, whilst the 'final comma' principle can be followed consistently with less risk of it, I personally vote for the latter.

Carey G V. 1958. *Mind the Stop: a brief guide to punctuation with a note on proof-correction*, p. 65. London: Penguin Books. 128 pp.

Canadian newspapers include mans-laughter, deter-gents, forest-all, gene-rations, and disc-over.

Conversely, use the non-breaking hyphen in words that you want to stay hyphenated. Use the combination Ctrl + Shift + hyphen or Alt + 0173 (typed through the numerical keypad with Num Lock on).

The serial (or Oxford) comma

Perhaps the most common use of commas is to separate three or more items in a series. Publishers are divided on the issue of whether to use a comma after the last-but-one items in the series, as that item is often followed by the word 'and', as in 'Red, green, and blue are the three primary colours'.

Most academic publishers use the serial comma, as it is generally known. Use it 'as default' but omit it when you want to indicate that the last two items are more closely related to each other than either of them is to any of the rest. For example, you may prefer not to use the serial comma in 'Costs include transport, installation, servicing and maintenance'.

References

Allen R. 2002
Punctuation
Oxford, UK: Oxford University Press. 104 pp.
[The book is part of the 'One step ahead' series 'for effective communication in everyday life.']

Carey G V. 1958
Mind the Stop: a brief guide to punctuation with a note on proof-correction
London: Penguin Books. 128 pp.

Kirkman J. 1999
Full Marks: advice on punctuation for scientific and technical writing, 3rd edn
Ramsbury, Wiltshire, UK: Ramsbury Books. 115 pp.

Trask L. 1997
The Penguin Guide to Punctuation
London: Penguin Books. 162 pp.

Chapter **13** What is the point?

Annexes A to D at a glance

Annexe A Specimen reference formats

Annexe B Authority for spellings
- References

Annexe C Observing, choosing, and using fonts
- What is a font?
- Observing fonts
- Choosing fonts
- Using fonts
- Some useful tips on using fonts on a PC
- Bibliography

Annexe D Formats for postal addresses and telephone numbers
- Formatting address blocks
- Style and format for mailing addresses
- Name and affiliation
- Address
- Criteria for machine-sortable mail
- Style for telephone and fax numbers
- References

A   Specimen reference formats

Formats that provide the bibliographic details of different types of documents – research papers published in journals, articles published in magazines and newspapers, books, individual chapters from books, web pages, and so on – are illustrated in this annexe; with appropriate modifications, they can be used for describing virtually any type of document. A few points of style common to all formats are as follows.

- Use the same typeface as that used for the main text but set the references in a font two points smaller. Reduce the line spacing accordingly.
- If space permits, split each reference into several lines; do not set the entire reference as one paragraph. In this system, some elements of a reference are always given a fresh line. Authors and year, for example, are given together in one line and the title of the document begins the next line.
- Invert the names of all authors, not just that of the first author (Pachauri R K *not* R K Pachauri) and separate the initials of authors with one space, not a full stop. However, insert a full stop and one space after the last initial of the last author to separate it from the year of publication.
- Use capitals sparingly: set the titles of papers, articles, and presentations as well as subtitles of books using sentence-style capitalization but use the 'title case' for titles of books, journals, and events (conferences, symposia, etc.).
- Mention inclusive page numbers (the first and the last page of a document). Insert an en dash (–), not a hyphen (-), between page numbers. Do not shorten page numbers to the least number of digits: 147–156 not 147-56.
- Supply the place of publication as well as the publisher for books, reports, and such non-periodical documents. Put the place of publication first and the publisher next, with a colon in between, as in London: Academic Press.

Specimens of 11 types of documents most commonly cited in technical literature are illustrated on the following pages.

Paper in a journal

> Fogarty L R , Haack S K, Wolcott M J, and Whitman R L. 2003
> **Abundance and characteristics of the recreational water quality indicator bacteria *Escherichia coli* and enterococci in gull faeces**
> *Journal of Applied Microbiology* **94**: 865–878

- Invert names of all authors (surname first, then initials).
- Set paper title in bold; follow sentence-style capitalization.
- Spell out journal title in full; set it in italics with 'title case' capitalization.
- Use en dash between page numbers.
- Set volume number in bold; skip issue number for journals.

Article in a magazine

> Dehaene S. 2003. **Natural born readers**
> *New Scientist* **179** (2402): 30–33 (5 July 2003)
> [Translated and adapted by Helen Phillips from the original in French]

- Include cover date for magazines.
- Include issue number; enclose it within brackets after volume number.

Chapter from a multi-authored volume

> Barnes M R and Southan C. 2003
> **Internet resources for the geneticist**, pp. 21–37
> in *Bioinformatics for Geneticists*, edited by M R Barnes and I C Gray
> Chichester, UK: Wiley. 408 pp.

- Set chapter title using sentence-style capitalization.
- Set volume title in italics using 'title case' capitalization.
- Do not invert names of editors.
- Give total number of pages in the volume as well.

Book

> Bell S and Morse S. 2003
> *Measuring Sustainability: learning from doing*
> London: Earthscan. 189 pp.
>
> - Include place of publication and publisher; separate the two by a colon followed by one space.
> - Mention the edition if other than first.

Presentation at a conference

> Panwar T S. 2001. Air pollution management in India
> Paper presented at the *Workshop on air pollution in the megacities of Asia* organized by the Korea Environment Institute
> Seoul, 3–5 September 2001.
>
> - Give the city and dates of the conference as well the organizer's name.

Report of a committee

> [Mashelkar] Committee on Auto Fuel Policy. 2002. Report of the expert committee on auto fuel policy, submitted to the Ministry of Petroleum and Natural Gas, Government of India. 298 pp.
>
> - Include chairperson's name; enclose it in square brackets.
> - Set titles of reports in sentence-case capitalization.
> - Mention the agency to which the report was submitted.

Ph.D. thesis

> Joshi V. 1981
> Application of energy-dispersive X-ray fluorescence technique for determination of the elemental composition of air particulate matter in Kanpur city
> Kanpur: Indian Institute of Technology. 62 pp. [Doctoral thesis submitted to the Dept of Physics]
>
> - Name the department within the degree-giving body.

Annexe **A** Specimen reference formats

A newspaper article

> Mohan N C. 2003
> Has the power of media declined?
> *The Financial Express*, New Delhi, 21 Aug. 2003: p. 6
>
> - Specify the city of publication. Include column number if appropriate.

Technical report

> McGee J. 1999
> Writing and designing print materials for beneficiaries: a guide for state medicaid agencies
> Baltimore, Maryland, USA: Health Care Financing Administration. 340 pp.
> [HCFA Publication No. 10145]
>
> - Use sentence-style capitalization for titles of reports.
> - Avoid using italics for titles.
> - Supply report number, project code, contract number, or similar identifying information.

A web page

> Barnes S. 2003. Help by subject: Writing and research.
> <www.library.ucsb.edu/subj/writ.html> [Accessed 7 Aug. 2003]
>
> - Enclose URL (uniform resource locator, or 'address' of the web page) within angled brackets.
> - Include the date of access.[a]

An e-mail message posted to a listserv

> Kessler E. 2003. 'Attachment' or 'Enclosure' with a fax?
> Message dated 5 Aug. 2003 posted to Copyediting-l, archived at http://listserv.indiana.edu/archives/copyediting-l.html [archive accessible only to subscribers]
>
> - Mention date of the message.
> - Include URL of the archives if available.

[a]All the URLs given in this book were accessed for confirmation on 16 and 17 September 2003.

B ▶ Authority for spellings

As proofreaders and copy editors know, their mistakes are immortalized in print, for everyone to see and for as long as the printed document survives. Errors of spelling are perhaps the ones most easily noticed. Therefore, these professionals take great care to ensure that words are correctly spelt. But what is correct? Consider the following pairs of words:
- analyse or analyze, adviser or advisor
- web site or website, database or data base
- by-product or byproduct, build-up or buildup
- forums or fora, auditoriums or auditoria
- Mao Tse Tung or Mao Zedong
- Mumbai or Bombay, Myanmar or Burma.

It is not always easy to come up with answers that satisfy everybody because correct spellings not only change with the region ('colour' in Britain, Australia, and Canada but 'color' in the US and the Philippines) but also with time (the first edition of the *Oxford Spelling Dictionary* (1986) had 'co-operation' but the second edition (1995) changed it to 'cooperation'; the 8th edition (1990) of the *Concise Oxford Dictionary* had 'rain forest' but the next edition (1995) changed it to 'rainforest').

Sometimes, spellings change because the system from which they were derived changes. For instance, when the official system for rendering Chinese names in English was changed from Wade–Giles to Pinyin, a slew of changes followed, including Mao Tse Tung to Mao Zedong and Peking to Beijing.

Plural forms of words from languages other than English also pose a problem when they are used in English texts: do we use the plural forms of such words in the original language or do we anglicize them in forming their plurals? Is it fora or forums, syllabi or syllabuses, termini or terminuses?

Address www.askoxford.com/asktheexperts/faq/usage/website

web site or website
It always takes a little time for new words to settle to a standardized form. Even our most recent dictionary, the revised 10th edition of the *Concise Oxford Dictionary*, published in 2001, shows web site, but it is now clear that the standard form is website, and future dictionaries will reflect this.

The US Board on Geographic Names adopted the change to Mumbai shortly after the Indian government did, but Randall Flynn, the board's executive secretary for foreign names, says either name is still okay—it just depends on your readers' familiarity with world politics. Flynn adds, 'If you're using one, you may want to include the other parenthetically, to cover all your bases.' ···

Dictionaries and other standard reference books are generally heading in the direction of Mumbai. Those whose most recent editions list this name first, with a second, parenthetical, or cross reference to Bombay, include *American Heritage*, *Webster's New World*, the Microsoft *Encarta*, *The World Almanac*, and the *National Geographic Atlas of the World*.

Wegman J. 2001. Summer in Mumbai? *Copy Editor* 12 (4): 6–7

The story is told (it is an invention but could be true) that a man born in those regions was asked: 'Where were you born?' 'In Hungary.' 'Where did you go school?' 'In Czechoslovakia.' 'Where did you go to high school?' 'In Hungary.' 'Where do you live now?' 'In the Soviet Union.' The other is duly impressed: you must have travelled a lot. 'Not at all. I never left Uzhorod.'

The town of Uzhorod (Ungvar) belonged to Hungary until 1918; then it became a part of Czechoslovakia; Hungary got it back after Munich but had to give it up to Soviet conquerors after World War Two. There is nothing very unusual in such stationary travelling in Central Europe.

Mikes G. 1973. *Any Souvenirs? Central Europe revisited*, p. 53. Harmondsworth, Middlesex, UK: Penguin Books. 192 pp.

Often, a choice has to be made between writing a term as two words, using a hyphen, and treating the term as a single word (post card, post-card, or postcard). Some pairs of words begin life in that form, acquire a hyphen as they come closer, and finally unite to form a single word. As communications become faster, the stage of hyphenation may be skipped altogether, as is likely with 'web site' (the current form as prescribed by the *New Oxford Dictionary of English* although 'website' is perhaps more common). How common the term is in a country is another factor: the *New Oxford Dictionary of English* gives 'sugar cane' whereas in India, 'sugarcane' is used almost exclusively.

Political developments often result in renaming of roads, streets, countries and even regions. For instance, Mount Road in Madras was renamed Anna Salai and Madras itself is now Chennai. Iran was Persia and Sri Lanka was Ceylon. At times, a single entity is split and only a part of that entity may carry the older name. For example, three new Indian states came into being on 1 November 2000: some districts of the state of Uttar Pradesh were separated from that state to form the new state of Uttaranchal; Chattisgarh was carved out of Madhya Pradesh; and the state of Bihar spawned Jharkhand.

Authority for spellings

In view of such variation, how does an editor decide on the correct spelling? The most commonly used approach is to specify one dictionary as the 'default' dictionary: if a word is defined in that dictionary, follow that spelling (including hyphenation and spacing). For TERI, the publishers of this handbook, that dictionary is NODE (*New Oxford Dictionary of English*), a comprehensive dictionary published in late 1998. The dictionary covers names of people and places as well. The new edition of the *Oxford Dictionary for Writers and Editors*, published in February 2000, supersedes NODE as the authority if the two do not match. For scientific and technical vocabulary, use the *Oxford Dictionary for Scientific Writers and Editors*, published in 1991.

> Address http://bmj.com/cgi/eletters/319/7225/1592#6018

> *Chamber's English Dictionary* defines foetus as 'the usual but etymologically unsatisfactory form of fetus', and the *Shorter Oxford English Dictionary* notes that 'the better form with e is rare except in US'. To have the support of two such reputable British dictionaries surely makes fetus a perfectly valid British spelling.
>
> Jacobs A. 1999. Re: hippy hangover?

> Spelling of names
> The publishers should use the same spellings for names as appearing on Survey of India maps. When in doubt about the spellings of names not appearing on Survey of India maps available for open circulation, the publishers may make a reference to the Regional Directors of Survey of India.
>
> Survey of India. 1987. *Instructions for publication of maps by central/state government departments/offices and private publishers*, p. 25. Dehra Dun, India: Survey of India. 37 pp.

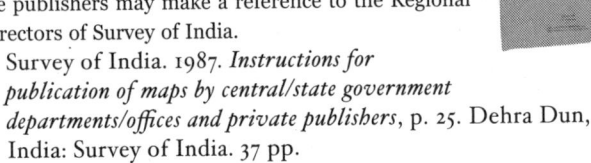

For scientific and technical terms not found in these dictionaries, indexes of abstracts journals are a good source. Because British spellings are the norm in India, journals from leading academic publishers from Britain are particularly useful. Appropriate discussion groups, including Copyediting-l, EASE-Forum, and Edline are yet another source of information.

Names of places often prove difficult and may have political implications. For Indian place names, the Survey of India suggests that current maps published by the Survey can be used as the authority. For names of places worldwide, an authoritative source is *The Times Comprehensive Atlas of the World*. The United Nations Group of Experts on Geographical Names, UNGEGN, brings together geographers, linguists, and historians from different geographical and linguistic divisions <http://www.un.org/Depts/unsd/cartog/index.htm>. The expert group holds its sessions three times during every five years; the most recent one was held in New York in January 2000. The United Nations Conference on the Standardization of Geographical Names was first held in Geneva in 1967 and has been held every five years thereafter; the most recent was in 2002.

Another handy source is the Getty Thesaurus of Geographic Names, a web site, which gives the latitude and longitude, a concise history, variant spellings with their sources, etc. of about 900 000 places worldwide.

The Times Comprehensive Atlas of the World lists over 225 000 place names.

References

The Concise Oxford Dictionary of Current English. 1990
8th edn, edited by R E Allen
Oxford, UK: Clarendon Press. 1454 pp.

The Concise Oxford Dictionary of Current English. 1995
9th edn, edited by D Thompson
Oxford, UK: Clarendon Press. 1454 pp.

The New Oxford Dictionary of English. 1998
Edited by J Pearsall
Oxford, UK: Clarendon Press. 2152 pp.

The Oxford Dictionary for Scientific Writers and Editors. 1991
Oxford, UK: Clarendon Press. 390 pp.

The Oxford Dictionary for Writers and Editors. 2000
2nd edn, edited and compiled by E M Ritter
Oxford, UK: Oxford University Press. 404 pp.

The Oxford Spelling Dictionary. 1986
Compiled by R E Allen
Oxford, UK: Oxford University Press. 300 pp.

The Oxford Spelling Dictionary. 1995
2nd edn, edited by M Waite
Oxford, UK: Clarendon Press. 624 pp.

The Times Comprehensive Atlas of the World. 1999
10th edn
London: Times Books. 220 pp.

C ▶ Observing, choosing, and using fonts

Names such as Times New Roman and Helvetica are now familiar to nearly all those who use a PC. Chances are that you have read dozens of documents that used Times or one of its clones—but how can you recognize that font? What are its distinguishing features? Do you remember the occasion when you opened a file only to be confronted by a mass of junk characters? And the cover page that you decked out in a snazzy font, full of bells and whistles, but which came out in a bland typewriter-like Courier? Are you so font savvy that you can tell Helvetica from Arial?

This annexe introduces you to the fascinating world of fonts and arms you with some basic information to prevent the more common problems encountered while using them.

What is a font?

A font is a set of instructions that tells a device (a computer monitor or a printer, for example) how to display each character: which dots to turn on and which dots to turn off, as it were. The observable differences in fonts – the presence or absence of serifs, for example – are a result of such instructions. Fonts are supplied as files, times.ttf, timesi.ttf, timesbd.ttf, and timesbi.ttf being the files for Times New Roman normal, italics, bold, and bold italics respectively in Windows. Start → Setting → Control Panel → Fonts will display the font files installed on the hard disk in Windows. The .ttf extension tells you that it is a TrueType font, the other common flavour being Type 1 or PostScript (with extensions .pfm and .pfb). The Windows operating systems prior to Windows 2000 required a separate software (such as Adobe Type Manager) for using Type 1 fonts.

For any font to be usable, the appropriate file must be available. The name of the font may be displayed in the format

Resource

Address: http://www.identifont.com/identify-sample.html

Identify a font

Identify a typeface by answering a series of simple questions about key features.

You may find it helpful to use a magnifying glass or hand lens if the text size is small.

Does the 'Q' tail cross the circle?
Ignore the shape of the tail.

- Q — Crosses the circle.
- Q — Touches the circle.
- Q — Below and separated from the circle.
- Q — Tail extends or lies inside circle.
- Q — Circle is open, tail part of same stroke.
- ? — Not sure.

Quote

Type design moves at the pace of the most conservative reader. The good type designer therefore realizes that, for a new fount to be successful, it has to be so good that only very few recognize its novelty. If readers do not notice the consummate reticence and rare discipline of a new type, it is probably a good letter. But if my friends think that the tail of my lower-case r or the lip of my lower-case e is rather jolly, you may know that the fount would have been better had neither been made. A type which is to have anything like a present, let alone a future, will neither be very 'different' nor very 'jolly'.

Morison S. 1967. *First Principles of Typography*, 2nd edn, pp. 7–8. Cambridge, UK: Cambridge University Press. 24 pp. [Cambridge Authors' and Printers' Guides 1]

Example

1234567890

MICR E13B font developed in 1958 by American Bankers Association for automatic cheque processing.

Identifying fonts by their characteristic features

bar but that does not necessarily mean that the font is available on the system. If the specified font is not available, it is substituted with another, but the substitute may or may not match the appearance of the intended font—this is one of the most common sources of annoyance.

Observing fonts

The most common habitat of fonts is a printed page, the next being the monitor of a PC. Fonts or, more precisely, typefaces, differ in many ways: for instance, some have serifs, the small cross-strokes at the ends of letters, whereas others – sans serif fonts – lack them. Just as you can recognize a known handwriting at a glance, though only a graphologist can point out the specific features that distinguish one hand from another, you can sense the differences among fonts but you may not be able to pin them down.

Typefaces are identified by such typical features: whether the letters have serifs at their ends (I versus l); whether the lower-case 'a' is 'single-storey' or 'two-storey' (ɑ and a); whether the dot in lower-case 'i' is round or square (i versus i); whether the cross-bar in 'e' is horizontal, slanted, or curved, and so on. A font is a subset or a particular instance of a typeface: Georgia is a typeface; 14-point Georgia Italic is a font. A useful starting point is <identifont.com/identify.html>, which helps you identify a font by drawing your attention to distinctive features of individual letters.

Such trivial differences can prove crucial at times. For instance, for e-mail addresses and Web addresses (URLs), the font must make a clear distinction between such similar-looking characters as the letter 'o' and the numeral zero; the letter 'g' and the numeral nine; a lower-case 'ell' (l), a capital 'eye' (I), and the numeral one (1); and so on. Sans serif fonts are often lacking on this count.

Apart from such differences, fonts also differ in other ways: some are larger, some are darker, some pack together compactly whereas some need more elbow room, and so on. Though

Annexe C Observing, choosing, and using fonts

Address http://members.aol.com/willadams/lucida.txt

Quote

Lucida Fax
Lucida Fax is a family of slab-serif fonts designed for telefaxing, dot-matrix printing, screen displays, and other situations where fonts must be rendered and reproduced at low resolutions or small sizes.
   Closely related to Lucida Bright, Lucida Fax has a large x-height, clear letter shapes, and open counters, but is more rugged, with heavier hairlines, thicker and shorter slab-shaped serifs, and greater space between letters. As its name implies, Lucida Fax is ideal for documents that will be telefaxed, from simple memos to complex newsletters.
   Bigelow C and Holmes K. 1997. Lucida family overview.

Quote

The telephone directory should be carefully designed to allow users to find the information they require quickly and accurately. Since it is essentially a massive list of names and numbers, and since using the directory involves the reader in scanning and reading the relevant individual entries, typefaces and layout are critical. It is however a lot to ask of any typeface
- to retain its looks in small size on thin, rough paper without being too difficult to print at extremely high speeds;
- to be economical of space on the page; and
- to be legible.

   Boag A. 1990. Bell Gothic & Bell Centennial. *Letterbox* 7: 4–5

Quote

It is wise to keep only one version of fonts that are identically or similarly named (e.g. TrueType AvantGarde and PostScript Avant Garde). It is very easy to mix them up, and they may not share the same metrics, which might easily disturb line endings and text flow. ···
   Do not forget that blank lines and invisible characters such as spaces and returns also have font and style names attributed to them. It is advisable to make a final check of all blank lines and invisibles ···
   Character sets may differ between Macintosh and Windows (e.g. ligatures) and font metrics may not be identical. If your file originated on another platform, get further proofs.
   Gordon B. 2001. *Making Digital Type Look Good*, pp. 34–35.
   New York: Watson-Guptill. 192 pp.

individually such differences are minute, their collective impact is substantial because a single page contains several thousand letters.

Choosing fonts

A major functional difference is the availability of different characters in a font. For general scientific work, we need such commonly used symbols as the degree symbol (°), a set of mathematical symbols (±, ×, etc.), a few Greek characters, and so on. Some fonts are entirely given over to special characters (Symbol and Wingdings, for instance). In this case, if the font is accidentally changed, you may end up getting junk characters.

The medium often influences the mode: some fonts (Georgia and Verdana, for example) are better for matter primarily meant to be read off a screen; some are especially suited for fax messages (Lucida Fax, for instance), some for posters, and some for OCR (optical character recognition). The code numbers printed on cheques (⑴ ⑵ ⑶ ⑷ ⑹) provide an example of a font that is particularly suited for MICR (magnetic ink character recognition). Letter Gothic was especially developed for overhead transparencies and Tiresias for TV displays. The numerals of Franklin Gothic Condensed are well designed, which makes the font a good choice for tables. If a document is likely to be photocopied through a generation or two (photocopy of a photocopy), you need to choose a font such as Georgia that retains its integrity in the process.

Using fonts

Though desktop publishing enables us to use dozens of fonts, it is better to limit the number in any one document lest it should end up looking like a catalogue of type specimens. Another consideration is portability: if a document is likely to go back and forth among users, it is best to stick to the most commonly available fonts, namely Times New Roman or its clones and Arial/Helvetica. A few other useful tips are given below.

Annexe C Observing, choosing, and using fonts

Some useful tips on using fonts on a PC

- In Windows, the sequence to load additional fonts is as follows: Start → Setting → Control Panel → Fonts → File → Install New Font, followed by specifying the path to the font file (drive and the folder).
- Carry the files of the fonts you have used along with the files of your PowerPoint presentations and install these fonts in the system you intend to use for the presentation. Alternatively, you may choose to embed the fonts: Save As → Tools → Embed TrueType Fonts. Be aware that licensing arrangements may restrict the fonts you can embed and that embedding makes files larger.
- Use fonts from trusted sources; corrupted font files do not show up immediately and can freeze a PC without warning. A zero-kilobyte font file indicates that the file is corrupt.
- Some fonts (bitmap fonts) are restricted to a particular size; that is, there may be a file for a font size of 10 points and a different one for 12 points. Such fonts cannot be enlarged or reduced in size.
- Keep in mind that special characters, symbols, etc., when inserted through the Insert→Symbol→Special Characters route, may not print correctly when the matter is pasted in another program (from Word to PowerPoint, for example).

Bibliography

Bringhust R. 1996
The Elements of Typographic Style, 2nd edn
Vancouver, Canada: Hartley & Marks. 350 pp.

Felici J. 2003
The Complete Manual of Typography: a guide to setting perfect type
Berkeley, California, USA: Peachpit Press. 361 pp.

Gordon B. 2001
Making Digital Type Look Good
New York: Watson-Guptill. 192 pp.

Heller S and Meggs P B (eds). 2001
Texts on Type: critical writings on typography
New York: Allworth Press. 275 pp.

D ▶ Formats for postal addresses and telephone numbers

The first bit of text that greets you when you receive anything by post is the postal address: if the name is misspelt, the sender has begun on the wrong foot; if the address is not error-free, the letter may not reach its destination at all or take too long to do so.

This annexe offers you a few guidelines on formatting postal addresses, both national and international, and answers questions such as those listed below.

▶ Is it necessary to add the name of the district if the address carries the PIN code (postal index number), the Indian postal code?
▶ How do I find out the PIN code of a place?
▶ Does Ms before a woman's name take a full stop?
▶ What are the recommended minimum margins while addressing envelopes?
▶ Where do I indicate the floor number within an address?

It is assumed that all addresses in a database are always entered from original sources such as letterheads, business cards, conference registration forms, and advertisements in the press—never from such secondary sources as other mailing lists and directories.

Formatting address blocks

Before we consider the details, we should consider the overall constraints on the address block as a whole, constraints imposed by the size of a typical mailing label or of the window of a window envelope, for instance. And if addresses are to be part of a database, there may well be restrictions on the number of lines and even on the number of characters for each of the elements of an address, such as name, title or designation, and affiliation. Mechanical sorting of mail, which involves 'reading'

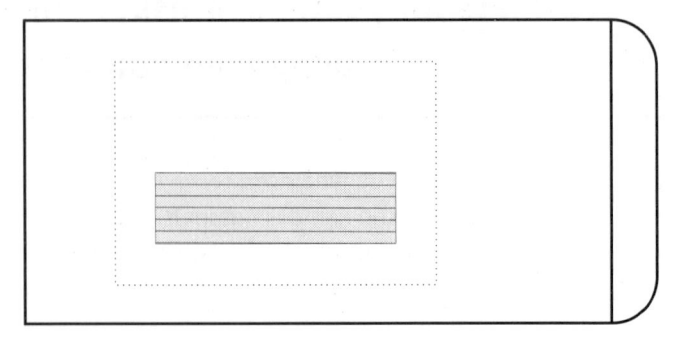

Type the address in a clear, open font (such as Courier New, Verdana, and Lucida Console) in 11 points with a line spacing of 12 points (6 lines to the inch or roughly 4 mm apart). Limit each line to 38 characters. Fit the address within 6 lines. Allow an extra line for foreign addresses.

Keep a clear area of at least 4 cm above the address block and at least 1.5 cm around the other three sides.

of each address by a machine, may well impose some special constraints of its own; for example, such a system will find it difficult to cope with cursive fonts that imitate handwriting.

Keep all addresses within 6 or fewer lines in all databases of addresses. For foreign addresses, you may allow one additional line. For printouts, use a clear and compact typeface: Verdana, Lucida Console, Courier New, or Andale Mono – all set in 10 points – work particularly well, with single-line spacing. Keep the width of the address block within 10 cm; the height will be approximately 3 cm so long as the address does not go beyond 7 lines in single-line spacing. The length of each line should not exceed 38 characters including spaces. Trim redundant information and edit each address using standard abbreviations to keep it within these limits.

The address block itself should be so placed as to leave a clear space of at least 4 cm at the top and 1.5 cm at the bottom. The top space is required for postage stamps and labels, postmarks, etc. whereas the bottom space is set aside for printing the bar code in the case of mechanically sorted mails. Also leave a clear area of at least 1.5 cm on either side of the address block. This clear area is referred to as the 'address detection area'.

Lists of addresses are often printed as part of conference proceedings, set it in 3 or 4 columns depending on the width of the page. This may mean that what would have fitted in a single line takes up two or more lines. If so, indent the second and subsequent lines (the 'turnover' lines). Set the names of participants in bold.

Style and format for mailing addresses

The Universal Postal Union's web site offers detailed information on the recommended address format for different countries. The Royal Mail advises that the two parts of the British postcode should be separated with one space and the postcode itself should be separated from any matter that comes

> The order of the address lines differs widely throughout the world. In many Western European and American countries, the address reads from top to bottom, and excluding the postal code, goes from the most specific at the top (the personal name) down to the least specific at the bottom (the postal town or province name). In many Eastern European countries, this is reversed, with the postal town or province name at the top and the personal name or street address at the bottom. ⋯ In some countries, no house-to-house deliveries exist. Deliveries are only made to postboxes or private bags. In other countries, only certain rural areas are not covered. As with many aspects of international data management, knowledge is the key to success when dealing with addresses.
>
> Rhind G. 2001. *Practical International Data Management: a guide to working with global names and addresses*, p. 113. Aldershot, Hampshire, UK: Gower. 179 pp.

```
New Delhi - 110 003
```

Separate the delivery post office and the pin code with an en dash with one space on either side of the dash

before it with at least two and preferably six spaces (Post Office 1978).

Rhind (2001) and Atkinson (1996) are more recent and comprehensive sources, as is the web page 'Effective Addressing for International Mail' maintained by Frank da Cruz <http://www.columbia.edu/kermit/postal.html>.

A typical address consists of a name (including a courtesy title such as Dr, Mr, Ms, etc.), a job title or designation, an affiliation, and a location. The name and location are essential elements; other elements may not apply in each case. Retired people, students, and freelancers, for example, may not carry a job title or affiliation. Every address should carry enough information (but not more) about its location for an article to be delivered there. In large organizations, such information may include a floor number or even a room number. In Indian cities, the name of the delivery post office is redundant if the PIN is included: 'Karol Bagh' is superfluous if the address includes 'New Delhi – 110 005' and 'Parel' is superfluous in 'Mumbai – 400 012'. For addresses in the US, the name of the state is superfluous if the address carries a ZIP code preceded by the 2-letter abbreviation for the state: if the address has 'Honolulu, HI 96822', Hawaii is redundant.

Here are a few points of style and format including those recommended by the Indian Department of Posts. It is assumed that the address block runs to no more than 6 lines, with the first line devoted to the addressee's name.

Name and affiliation

- Always use a courtesy title (Dr, Mr, Ms, etc.) before the name. Please note that Dr, Mr, Ms, and Mrs do not end with a full stop. However, do not include academic degrees and such affiliations as IAS (Indian Administrative Service) and IFS (Indian Forest/Foreign Service).
- Separate initials in names with single spaces, not full stops.
- Include the name of a smaller unit (department, section, cell, unit, etc.) within a large organization as appropriate. At

| Address | http://www.indiapost.org/Netscape/Pincode.html |

What is a PIN code?

The 6-digit post code used in India is referred to as the PIN (postal index number) code. The first digit indicates the region; the first two digits together indicate the sub-region or one of the postal circles; and the first three digits together indicate the sorting or revenue district. The last three digits refer to the delivery post office.

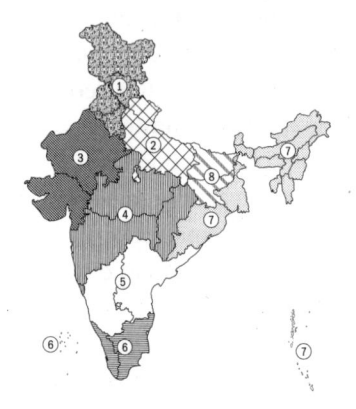

The first digit of the PIN indicates a region.

The first two digits of the PIN code indicate a sub-region or a postal circle.

11	Delhi
12 and 13	Haryana
14 to 16	Punjab
17	Himachal Pradesh
18 to 19	Jammu and Kashmir
20 to 28	Uttar Pradesh (including Uttaranchal)
30 to 34	Rajasthan
36 to 39	Gujarat
40 to 44	Maharashtra
45 to 49	Madhya Pradesh (including Chattisgarh)
50 to 53	Andhra Pradesh
56 to 59	Karnataka
60 to 64	Tamil Nadu
67 to 69	Kerala
70 to 74	West Bengal
75 to 77	Orissa
78	Assam
79	North-eastern states other than Assam
80 to 85	Bihar (including Jharkhand)

times, the designation or job title itself will indicate such a sub-unit.
- Use acronyms instead of spelling out an organization's name in full.
- Ensure that an organization's name is correctly spelt if you decide to spell it out; it should reflect the organization's preference where alternative spellings and hyphenation are possible. The OECD (Organization for Economic Co-operation and Development), for instance, hyphenates cooperation and PricewaterhouseCoopers is a single word with mixed capitalization.

Address

- Exclude from the address such directions as 'Opposite Liberty Cinema' or 'Behind petrol pump'; in most cases, they can be safely omitted.
- Exclude from all post-box or post-bag addresses such details as the house number, name of the street or road, and name of the area—the post box number, name of the post office, and the PIN code are the only items required for such addresses.
- Enclose the floor number in brackets and place it immediately after the name of the building, as in 'Piramal Towers (2nd floor). If unavoidable, abbreviate floor to fl. (note the dot).
- Prefer arabic numbers to roman numbers no matter how they are shown in the original source.
- Keep punctuation to the minimum. Do not separate the house number from the name of a street or road, as in 65 Davies Street or 8 Khanapur Road.
- End every Indian address with a PIN code. Exclude names of districts or states so long as addresses carry PIN codes. Assign a separate line to the delivery post office and the PIN code: both appear in one line and are separated by an en dash with a single space before and after.

Annexe **D** Formats for postal addresses and telephone numbers

Address: www.indiapost.org/Netscape/pinsearch1.asp

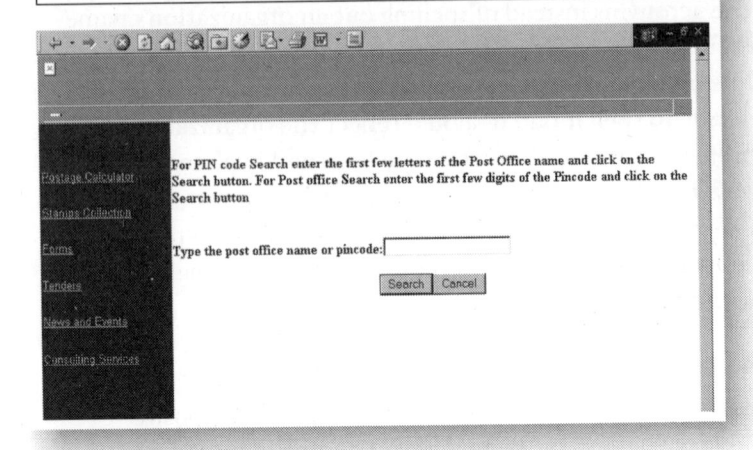

Resource

For PIN code Search enter the first few letters of the Post Office name and click on the Search button. For Post office Search enter the first few digits of the Pincode and click on the Search button

Type the post office name or pincode:

[Search] [Cancel]

- Postage Calculator
- Stamps Collection
- Forms
- Tenders
- News and Events
- Consulting Services

Whenever you post MAIL, make it.....
MACHINEABLE

The Department of Posts has introduced computerised letter sorting machines for efficient sorting of mail. Mail should be compatible with the machine. Follow the following

IT'S RIGHT TO BE LIGHT
Use white or relatively light coloured envelopes.

PASTE IN HASTE IS WASTE
Use only glue to close all flaps of lettercard & envelope properly.

BOX 'N' CODES
Complete the address with Postal Index Number (PIN).

EQUALITY GIVES QUALITY
Use envelope of the right size for the contents. Ensure that the inside matter fills in the envelope. Maximum permissible margin is 15 mm in length & 10 mm in width.

MARGINS ARE IN
Leave a 15 mm margin from the bottom edge for Bar coding, free of everything : address label, writing and so on.

METAL IS LETHAL
Don't use staplers to close the envelope as metal pins may damage the system.

AIR TIGHT IS RIGHT
On window envelopes, ensure that the transparent portion of the window is firmly glued and the address clearly and fully visible.

NO RIGID OBJECT
No hard, rigid or semi-rigid object inside as it is not accepted by the machine.

Facilitating machine sorting of mail

Print the PIN code as two groups of 3 digits each, separated by a space. Use the PIN code directory or the web page <http://www.indiapost.org/pincode.htm> maintained by the Department of Posts to find out the correct PIN code.

‣ End every foreign address with the name of the country, with or without a post code as appropriate. Make the name of the country conform to that in a list available at the web site of the Universal Postal Union <www.upu.int/upu/AN/Pays_membres.html >

Criteria for machine-sortable mail

The Department of Posts uses automatic sorting machines for quicker handling and delivery of mail. Every piece of mail must meet each of the following criteria so that it can be easily machine-sorted.

Colour Use white or any light-coloured envelopes. The colour should be even and without any design or pattern such as those commonly found in hand-made paper. The envelope should be opaque.

Fasteners Seal envelopes with glue. Avoid staples, pins, clips, button-and-string, and other such fasteners to seal envelopes. Keep even the contents of envelopes free of these fasteners.

Weight and thickness Keep the weight of the mailing piece (envelope and contents) within 50 g and its thickness within 5 mm.

Space within an envelope Ensure that the contents fit snugly within the envelope. The dimensions of the contents, whether folded or unfolded, should be only 5 to 10 mm smaller than the corresponding dimensions of the envelope.

Style for telephone and fax numbers

The style for such items of information as telephone numbers and postal codes should represent their underlying structure. Take a typical 7-digit telephone number, for example: its first 3 digits represent the exchange; accordingly, these are separated

Address | http://www.wtng.info/wtng-glo.html

Telephone numbering terminology
An **area code** is used within a country to route calls to a particular city, region or special service. Depending on the country or region, it may also be referred to as a numbering plan area, subscriber trunk dialling code, national destination code, or routing code.

A **country code** is used to reach the particular telephone system for each country or special service. A plus sign (+) is usually placed before a country code (+91 is India, for instance) to indicate the code to initiate international calls (usually 00, but it is not the same for every country)

A **trunk prefix** refers to the initial digit(s) to be dialled in a domestic call, prior to the area code (if necessary) and the subscriber number. 0 is the trunk prefix in most countries. For calls to another country code, the trunk prefix is generally omitted.

A **geographic area code** refers to an area code that has a defined geographic boundary. Geographic area codes are for conventional fixed-line (or land line) services terminating at fixed points. Non-geographic area codes would include wireless (cellular and pager whose subscribers could be located at variable points), or toll-free services (usually assignable on a nation-wide basis, without being bound to specific regions).

The **local number** or subscriber number represents the specific telephone number to be dialed, but does not include the country code, area code (if applicable), international prefix or trunk prefix.

Recommended grouping of digits in telephone and fax numbers

Total number of digits	Grouping	Example
4 or fewer	— (printed as a single group)	1234
5	2 + 3	12 345
6	2 + 4	12 3456
7	3 + 4	123 4567
8	4 + 4	1234 5678

from the remaining 4 digits with a space, as in 468 2111. In 6- and 5-digit telephone numbers, the first two digits represent the exchange. In the PIN code, on the other hand, the first 3 digits identify the sorting district and the last 3 digits pinpoint the delivery post office within the sorting district; therefore, the gap appears between the first 3 digits and the last 3 digits.

Delhi, Mumbai, and many other Indian cities now have 8-digit local telephone numbers. Print these with a space after the first 4 digits, as in 2468 2111.

The international format for telephone numbers includes the country code in addition to the any other code required for long-distance calls within a country (known as the STD or subscriber trunk dialling code in India), as in +91 11 2468 2111 where the plus sign indicates the code used to access international dialling (which may vary from country to country), 91 is the country code for India, and 11 is the city (area) code for Delhi, followed by a local 8-digit telephone number. Set all fax numbers the same way as telephone numbers.

Here are a few reminders on setting contact details.
- Ensure that the numbers are correct and current.
- Give only the local numbers when only local calls are expected. Give the STD code preceded by a zero (011 for Delhi, 080 for Bangalore, etc.) if you expect long-distance (but not international) calls. The international format excludes the zero but includes a country code preceded by the plus sign, as illustrated here: +91 11 2468 2111 (followed by 'extn' and the appropriate extension number, if any).
- Separate alternative numbers with 'or' instead of a slash, as in 2468 2111 or 2468 2100; the slash may be mistaken for the numeral one (1) especially if set close.
- Use a typeface with clear numerals; Franklin Gothic Condensed is the first choice but Officina, Verdana, and Georgia also work well.
- Avoid giving telephone and fax numbers one after the other; the numbers share a similar structure and a mix-up is possible. Insert an e-mail address between the telephone and fax numbers where appropriate.

Annexe **D** Formats for postal addresses and telephone numbers

> | ✗ | ✗ | ✗ | ✗ | ✓ | Example
> | 'phone | ph | Ph | Tel | Tel. |
>
> Shorten 'Telephone' to 'Tel.' if necessary

- Shorten Telephone to Tel. (note the dot) if necessary.
- Set such labels as Tel., Fax, and E-mail in bold.
- Prefer Web to web site, URL, or home page as a label. Omit http// when giving URLs (uniform resource locators).

References

Atkinson T D. 1996
Merriam-Webster's Guide to International Business Communications, 2nd edn
Springfield, Massachusetts, USA: Merriam-Webster. 412 pp.

Post Office. 1978
London Post Offices and Streets
London: HMSO. 244 pp.

Rhind G. 2001
Practical International Data Management: *a guide to working with global names and addresses*
Aldershot, Hampshire, UK: Gower. 179 pp.
<http://www.grcdi.nl/products.htm#data>

Index

Excludes quotes, examples, resources, and other similar items that appear on left-hand pages.

abbreviations 47–61
  ambiguous 11
  apostrophe in 57
  capitals in spelt-out versions 57
  and contractions, difference between 9
  of currencies 73
  definition 63
  explaining 53, 55
  full stops in 9
  of names of organizations in references 53
  of non-English terms 59
  plurals 57
  pronunciation 49
  spacing of letters in 59
  and spelt-out versions, which comes first 55
  and symbols, difference between 63
  of titles of journals 145
  types 49, 51
  typographic refinements 59, 61
acronyms
  attaining the status of regular words 47
  preceded by 'a' or 'an' 49
AD, before the year 67
alignment
  of numbers in a column 89
  of numbers in numbered headings 29
  of row headings with rest of the row
  vertical, of multi-line column headings
American and British usage, differences in 7
  complimentary close, in letters 157
  salutation, in letters 7
  spellings 13
  thousands separator 65
apostrophe
  in plurals of abbreviations 211
arabic numerals
  in postal addresses 237
  preferred to roman numerals 5
ASCII characters, in e-mails 161
author–year system (of citing references) 131, 133

BC, after the year 67
bibliographic details
  used by publishers 215
  recording 127
BMP files 119
bullet points *see* lists

camel case 57
capitals
  book titles 215
  in headings 23
  names of conferences 215
  in spelt-out version of abbreviations 57, 59
  table titles 83
  titles of articles, papers, presentations 215
  for units of measurement named after persons
  use of 13, 57
  see also small capitals
captions, for figures 121
charts
  3-dimensional 115
  hierarchy of lines in 113
  labels for axes in 111

charts (cont.)
  labels for curves, bars, segments 111
  labels 115
  leader lines 115
  patterns for filling bars and segments 113
  patterns for lines 115
  as presentation visuals 177
  shades of grey as fills 113
  size of lettering 109
  thickness of lines in 109
  types 107
Chicago Manual of Style 13
citation formats
  articles in magazines 216
  articles in newspapers 218
  books 217
  conference proceedings 129, 131
  e-mail messages 218
  presentations at conferences 217
  reports of committees 217
  specimens of **215–218**
  technical reports 218
  theses 131, 217
  web pages 218
CMYK format for colours 119
colon
  in ratios 209
  in references 147
  following a salutation
  in time of the day
  after verbs 211
colour
  CMYK format 119
  in posters 183
  in presentation visuals 175
  RGB format 119
column headings (in tables)
  abbreviations 87
  alignment of numbers 87
  multipliers 87
  spanner rules 87
  vertical alignment 87
comma
  before 'and' in a series 213
  in citations 209
  in dates 209
  as decimal marker 65

  in postal addresses 237
  in references, use of 147
Concise Oxford Dictionary 219
contractions
  and abbreviations, difference between 9
  formation 51
  use of full stops after 51
crores, conversion to millions 65
currency
  3-letter codes 73, 163
  abbreviations 73
  symbols 73

dashes, as item-markers in lists 37
  see also em dash, en dash
data sources in tables 93
dates
  format 3, 67
  leading zero in 3, 67
degree sign 73
dictionaries
  Concise Oxford Dictionary 219
  New Oxford Dictionary of English 13, 57, 221
  Oxford Dictionary for Writers and Editors 221
  Oxford Dictionary for Scientific Writers and Editors 221
  Oxford Spelling Dictionary 219
disk files
  bullet points in 199
  file extensions of 197
  footnotes in 199
  formatting of 199
  graphics (illustrations) in 201
  labelling of 201, 203
  management of 199
  marking paragraphs in 201
  naming 197, 199, 203
  non-ASCII characters in 199
  in PDF 197
  preparation of 195
  special characters in 199
documents, usability of 5

electronic files *see* disk files
em dash 39, 91, 211

em space 39
e-mail addresses, choice of fonts 3
e-mails
　ASCII characters in 161
　attachments to 163
　confidentiality 163
　format 161
　line length 161
　salutation and complimentary close 163
　signature files 161
　subject field 161
　substitute for boldface in 163
　substitute for italics in 163
embedded lists (run-on lists) 33
en dash 73, 211
　pairs of, as parentheses 73
　between page numbers 147, 215
en space 39
endnotes 141
EPS files 119
et al.
　with four or more authors 133
　italics or roman 135
　versus 'and others' 133

fax messages, formatting 159
file extensions 197
file formats
　CMYK 119
　EPS files 119
　GIF 121
　JPEG 107, 119, 121
　PDF 197
　RGB 119
　TIFF 107, 119
file names, system for 197, 199
fonts **225–230**
　bitmap 230
　for computer screens 11
　contrast between normal and bold 11
　for different applications 229
　for e-mail addresses
　for fax messages 159
　installation in Windows 230
　MICR (magnetic ink character recognition) 229

OCR (optical character recognition) 229
　for postal addresses 233
　PostScript 225
　sans serif 227
　size of 11
　size for reference lists 215
　TrueType 225
　for URLs 3, 227
footnotes 141
　choice of symbols 141
　sequence of markers 93
　in tables 91
formats for references 215
　see also citation formats
full stop
　in abbreviations 9
　after contractions 51
　omitting in contractions 9
　preceding a footnote marker 209
　in references 147

geographic coordinates, notation for 73
GIF files 121
graphs *see* charts

Harvard system of citation *see* author–year system
headings **15–31**
　capitalization 23
　choice of words in 17
　extended into margins 31
　font size in relation to page size 29
　functions of 17
　hierarchy of 15, 19
　indent for the line following 25
　indented 27
　length of 31
　levels of 17, 19
　line-breaks in 25
　minimum number of lines to follow 23
　numbered 27, 29
　numbering of 15
　parallel structure in 17

Index

headings (cont.)
  punctuation in 15, 23
  run-on, closing punctuation 25
  sense-lining 25
  separate columns for, in tables 31
  space above and below 21, 23
  underlining 31
headnote, in tables 85
home page, in addresses 242
hour, symbol for 71
hyphen
  non-breaking 213
  at ends of lines 211
hyphenation rules, changes with
    time 219, 221

illustrations **103–123**
  35-mm slides 115
  functions of 105
  line and tone 107
  photographs 115
  positioning 121
  size 109
  types 105
indent
  hanging
  for the line following a heading 27
  for the line of text after a list 43
  negative 31
  in titles of tables 85
initialisms 49
inverted commas *see* quotation
    marks
item marker in lists, choice of 37

JPEG files 107, 119, 121
justification, full versus left 9

labels
  for axes in graphs 9
  for disk files 201, 203
  for figures *see* captions
lakhs, conversion to millions 65
landscape tables, positioning on a
    page 99
latitude, notation 73

leading zero in dates 3, 67
legibility
  of fonts on computer screens 11
  constraints to 169
letters
  'cc' (carbon copy) 159
  complimentary close 157
  continuation sheets 159
  date format and position 157
  enclosures 157
  inside address 157
  layout 155
  salutation 157
  subject line 157
levels of headings, judgement in
    assigning 27
line illustrations, scanning of 119
line spacing
  in postal addresses 233
  in typescripts
lines (rules) in designing tables 9
listening versus reading 165
lists **33–45**
  displayed versus run-on 33
  formatting of bullet points 37
  length 35, 43
  punctuation 35, 41
  run-on (embedded) 35
  space above and below 41
litres
  abbreviation of 65
  spelling out in full 69
longitude, notation 73

mail, machine sorting of 239
manuscripts **187–203**
  binding 189
  choice of paper 191
  citation of references 193
  covering letter 193
  formatting 189
  identifying information 191
  layout in columns in 191
  legal release 193
  line spacing 189
  mailing 195
  margins 189
  packing 195

Index

manuscripts

page numbers 191
submission to journals 187
measurement, choice of units 63
millions, preferred to lakhs 65
missing values in cells of a table 91
mixed capitalization 57
mixed case *see* mixed capitalization
multiplication sign 73

negative exponent, in expression of physical quantities 65
negative indent 31
nested lists 39
New Oxford Dictionary of English 13, 57, 221
non-breaking hyphen 213
non-breaking space 67, 71
number of authors in references 135
numbered headings 27
   alignment 29
   for cross-referencing 29
   separate column for numbers 29
   typography 29
Numbered references 131
numbers
   general **65–67**
   rounding off 79
numerals
   arabic versus roman 5
   similar in appearance to alphabets 3, 227

overhead transparencies 169
   legibility when projected 173
   in presentations, aspect ratio of 173
   templates 173
Oxford Dictionary for Scientific Writers and Editors 221
Oxford Dictionary for Writers and Editors 221
Oxford Spelling Dictionary 219

page layouts, principles 21
parallel structure
   for items in a list 37

in headings 17
parallelism *see* parallel structure
parentheses, in references 147
Pascal case 57
PDF (portable document format), preparing 197
per cent sign 67
photographs
   care 117
   editing 117
   handling 117
   indication of orientation 117
   labelling 117
   packing 117, 195
   photocopying 115
   scanning 119
PIN code (Indian postal code) 237, 239, 241
'pipe' (special character) 163
place names
   changes in 221
   sources of information 223
plurals
   of abbreviations 57
   of non-English words 219
postal addresses **231–239**
   fonts for 233
   formatting 231, 233
   length of lines in 233
   line spacing 233
   number of lines in 233
   size of address block in 233
   writing of 237
Postcode (UK), format 233
posters **179–185**
   colour 183
   contents 181
   reading contrasted with viewing 179
   sessions at conferences, participation in 183, 185
   size and layout 181
   size of lettering 181
   supplies for mounting 183
   'tiling' 181
   title 181
PowerPoint
   file size 175
   template 175

Index

presentation visuals
  charts 177
  colour 175
presentations **165–177**
  aims 169
  allowing audience time to read 175
  formats of visual aids 169
  length 169
  using a PC 169, 171
  visibility of projected material 173
  see also screen shows
pronouns, antecedents in
    headings 17
pronunciation of abbreviated
    forms 49
punctuation **205–213**
  changes with time 207
  in headings 23, 25
  in lists 35, 41
  purpose 205
  reference citations within text 139
  in salutation in letters
    to separate parts of a
    reference 145, 147
  in titles of tables 83
  verbs 211
  see also under specific punctuation
    marks
physical quantities, notation for 7

question mark 209
quotation marks, single or
    double 209

raised dot 9
reading, contrasted with
    listening 165
references
  and bibliography, difference
    between 143
  alphabetic arrangement 143
  authors with same surnames 135
  author–year (Harvard) system 131
  boldface in 149
  capitalization of titles 149
  citing documents at second-
    hand 139

following a journal's style 193
  functions 127
  identical author–year
    combinations 135
  italics 149
  names of authors in 145
  national usages for names 145
  numbered (Vancouver
    system) 131, 133
  organization as author 137
  punctuation in citations 139
  separate lines for different
    elements 149
  shortening forenames of authors
    to initials 145
  unpublished sources 139
resolution, for scanning 107
RGB colour format 119
roman numerals
  in numbered lists 37
  versus arabic numerals 5

salutation in letters, followed by
    colon or comma 7
sans serif (fonts) 227
scanning
  line illustrations 119
  photographs 119
screen shows
  aspect ratio 173
  colour contrast 175
  transitions 175
  animations 175
semicolon, in run-on lists 209
serial comma 213
serifs 227
SI units 67
slash
  use in financial years 207
  with physical quantities 9
slides, 35-mm 115
  checking legibility when
    projected 173
  PowerPoint 177
  in presentations 169
  printing of 119
small capitals 61

space
  above and below headings 21, 23
  above and below a list 41
  after run-on headings 25
  around address blocks 233
  around bullet points 39
  around en dash 211
  before question mark 209
  between characters in fax
    messages 159
  between letters in
    abbreviations 59
  between words 9
  with colon in ratios 209
  in expressions of physical
    quantitics 9
  in large (multi-digit) numbers 65
  see also non-breaking space
special characters 71
  in disk files 199
  see also degree symbol, em dash,
    em space, en dash, en space,
    non-breaking hyphen, non-
    breaking space, pipe
spelling rules, changes with time 219
spellings
  authority for 221
  British and American 13
square brackets, in references 147
stem sentence 41
stub, in tables 85
style
  definition 3
  essentials of 9
  need for 7
style guides and manuals 5, 7
symbols
  versus abbreviations 63
  definition 63
  prefixes 69
  repetition of 71
  plural forms 49, 51, 69
  of units of measurement named
    after persons 69

tables 75–101
  choice of footnote symbols 91
  column headings 85
  'continued' line in 99
  design and format 95
  footnotes 91
  gaps between columns 95
  heading for the stub 85
  headnotes 85
  'landscape' (wide) 99
  numbering of, in annexes or
    appendixes 83
  mention in text 79
  notation for missing values 91
  numbering 5, 79
  organization of data in 77, 79
  oversized 101
  positioning within text blocks 97
  scheme for numbering 81, 83
  sequence of footnotes 93
  sequence of rows and columns 79
  sources of data 93
  split across pages 99
  titles 83
  units of measurement in row
    headings 89
  unnumbered (informal or
    open) 77
  vertical and horizontal rules in 95
technical documents, reading of 15
telephone, abbreviation of 242
telephone numbers
  grouping of digits in 241
  international format 241
  styling 239
templates
  for 35-mm slides 177
  for overhead transparencies 173
  for PowerPoint presentations 175
TERI (The Energy and Resources
    Institute) 3
thousands separator 65
  use in four-digit numbers 67
TIFF files 107, 119
time, format for 67, 69
typefaces and fonts, difference
    between 227
typescripts *see* manuscripts
typographic refinements, in lists 43,
    45

units of measurement
  in table titles 83
  in industry and commerce 71
  choice of 63
  repetition of 71
usage, British versus American *see* American and British usage, differences in
user-friendly design 11

Vancouver system of citation 131, 133

word spacing, uniformity in 9
World Bank Publications Style Manual 7

x-height 181

years
  format for 67
  placement of AD and BC 67

ZIP code 235